Ringneck Parakeets

GW00671250

**The Complete Owner's Guide
to Ringneck Parakeets**

Including Indian Ringneck Parakeets, their Care,
Breeding, Training, Food, Lifespan, Mutations,
Talking, Cages and Diet

Foreword

Hello and thank you for buying my book.

In this book you will find some wonderful information to help you care for your Ringneck Parakeets. I've included in this book information about care, habitat, cages, enclosure, diet, facts, set up, food, names, pictures, life span, breeding, feeding cost and a care sheet.

I have written this book using American spelling as that is what I'm used to. I have given measurements in both feet and inches/pounds and ounces and also in metric. I have also given costs in US$ and GBP. Both the measurements and costs are approximate guides. I have done my best to ensure the accuracy of the information in this book as at the time of publication.

I trust that after reading this book you will enjoy the experience of owning and looking after a Ringneck Parakeet and that you have a wonderful time enjoying the pleasure they bring in the years to come!

All good wishes,

Rose Sullivan

Ringneck Parakeets

The moral rights of the author has been asserted

British Library Cataloguing in Publication Data

A catalogue record for this book is available from the British Library

ISBN 978-1-909820-13-5

Disclaimer and Legal Notice

Acknowledgements

I would like to extend my sincerest thanks to my dear friend Katherine for all her input in assisting me put this book together. She has long experience of looking after Ringneck Parakeets and without her feedback I'm sure I'd have missed something.

I must also thank my husband Marc and our children Mike and Cathy for their love and patience as mom taps away on her computer. Their understanding and love for my passion made the whole journey worthwhile.

Table of Contents

Commonly Used Terms

aviary - A facility where birds are bred for enjoyment and sale, or an outside enclosed structure where birds are housed.

aviculture - The process of keeping pet birds as companions.

beak - The upper and lower mandible or jaw of a bird that in Ringneck Parakeets has a hooked shape.

bird safe - An enclosed environment including a room or aviary that has been cleared of hazards and has no means of escape. Suitable for a companion bird to free fly.

bluffing - Aggressive and anti-social behavior seen in adolescent Ringneck Parakeets. Essentially avian puberty. Resolves in four months to one year.

cage - The primary secure habitat in which a companion bird lives for its security and well-being.

companion bird - Also referred to as a pet bird. Any bird, like a Ringneck Parakeet that lives with and interacts with humans on a daily basis.

crop - A sac located between the esophagus and stomach of a bird that serves to hold food for preliminary digestion.

cuttlebone - A pumice-like chew toy given to companion birds as a source of calcium and a means of wearing down the animal's beak.

feather - The flat appendages that form a bird's plumage, including the ten long flight feathers on the wings.

free flying - The practice of allowing a companion bird time outside its cage to fly uninhibited in a bird safe environment.

hand-rearing - The process of raising a bird from infancy by hand to acclimate it to human contact.

parakeet - Long-tailed parrots such as the Ringneck Parakeet.

veterinarian - A medical professional trained in the treatment of animals commonly referred to as a vet. A veterinarian who specializes in birds is an avian veterinarian.

zoonotic – A disease that can be transmitted from an animal to a human being.

Chapter 1 - Introduction

Whether they are called Ringneck Parakeets, Indian Ringneck Parakeets or Rose-Ring Parakeets, these birds are the only naturalized parakeet in the United Kingdom and Europeans have kept the birds as pets since the time of Alexander the Great.

These beautiful creatures are friendly and easily tamed, with something of a rakish sense of humor. People who are new to aviculture are amazed at the range of emotions a Ringneck Parakeet can convey, especially once it begins to acquire a vocabulary and talk.

A parakeet is, after all, simply a long-tailed parrot. They make excellent companions, thriving on a busy family environment and happily chiming in with their own two cents worth on whatever happens to be going on around them.

While certainly not the loudest companion bird, your Ringneck will make plenty of noise, which is something to consider before you welcome one into your home as a pet.

Mimicking their wild cousins, pet Ringneck Parakeets are most active at dawn and dusk, often serving as highly efficient alarm clocks for their owners.

Human beings keep animals for many reasons. Even dogs and cats became domesticated because there was a potential for a mutually beneficial relationship with people.

Dogs perform a wide range of jobs for man from herding and protecting livestock, to tracking game, and assisting in law enforcement. Some dogs have even been trained to detect the onset of a seizure and go to the person's aid.

Cats began to live with humans to control small vermin, performing a vital function in preserving food supplies and curtailing the spread of disease.

Poultry like chickens and turkeys supply eggs, and are a source of meat.

But what of a bird like a parakeet? These creatures are kept solely for their beauty, beguiling charm, and companionship. They serve no function but to provide company and pleasure.

To some people keeping a bird, like maintaining an elaborate tank of fish, seems like too much work for animals that don't fetch a ball or sit contentedly on your lap purring.

Aquarists and aviculturists would beg to differ about their relationship with their unique pets. Unquestionably Ringneck Parakeets are affectionate, devoted and loyal.

With a lifespan often reaching 20 years, a Ringneck Parakeet will truly become a member of the family.

The birds exhibit excellent memory, and recognize and greet family members who have been absent for a period of time, for instance a grown child returning home after a long semester at college.

Parakeets have distinct personalities, definite likes and dislikes, and an expressive ability to get their point across. Simply put, if you've never lived with one, you're in for a real adventure!

There are approximately 330 species of parrots living in the world today. Of those, the Ringneck Parakeet (also known as the Indian Ringneck Parakeet or the Rose-Ring Parakeet) has the widest distribution. A parakeet is simply a parrot with a long tail.

These colorful and gregarious birds can be found across Asia and China, in Africa, high up in the Himalayas and even around major cities in Europe and Great Britain.

History and Origin

The Ringneck Parakeet was the first parrot to be kept widely as a pet by Europeans, making its way to Greece in 327 BC with the armies of Alexander the Great.

The birds enjoyed high favor with the Romans, who housed them in cages inlaid with ivory and precious jewels and assigned slaves to care for the parakeets and to teach them to talk.

Ringneck Parakeets have been popular pets in the UK since Victorian times, and there are now established wild populations in southeastern England.

The first Ringneck Parakeet to be reported living in the wild in the UK was found in Kent in 1969. Now the population in England is thought to exceed 40,000.

The feral Ringneck Parakeets in Britain are the largest population of wild parrots to live so far north, but since the birds have been reported all the way to the borders of Wales and Scotland they are continuing to spread.

There are also feral colonies of Ringnecks in the United States, the Middle East, the Netherlands, Germany, Paris, Rome, Lisbon and even the Himalayas among other locations. In their native Asia and Africa the birds are considered to be agricultural pests, wreaking havoc on crops.

Ringneck Parakeets are in no danger of extinction, having been given "Least Concern" status by The International Union for the Conservation of Nature.

However, in areas where feral populations are well established, concern has been expressed — sometimes vigorously — about the pressure Ringneck Parakeets may exert on native species.

Regardless, these birds remain highly desirable as pets and are well loved by enthusiasts both in their captive and wild state.

Physical Description

Ringneck Parakeets are fairly large, averaging 15.6 inches (39.6 centimeters) in length, with a wingspan of 17.7 inches (45 centimeters). Adults weigh 4.1 to 5 ounces (116 to 142 grams). They are very vocal birds and in captivity can learn to speak. Ringnecks emit a wide range of sounds from shrieks to whistles, and will call during flight.

There are four recognized subspecies:

African Ringneck Parakeet (P.k. krameri)

Males of the African Ringneck Parakeet (P.k. krameri) subspecies are generally green or yellow with black chins and broad black stripes across the lower check. A pink collar encircles the neck, with the nape of the neck washed in blue.

The bird's upper mandible is dark red and tipped with black, while the lower mandible is black with a dark red base.

Abyssinian Ringneck Parakeet (P.k. parvirostris)

In the Abyssinian Ringneck Parakeet (P.k. parvirostris) subspecies, the head and cheeks will be greener. The birds have smaller bills that are a brighter red.

Indian Ringneck Parakeet (P.k. manillensis)

The Indian Ringneck Parakeet (P.k. manillensis is somewhat larger, with black lower mandibles and more pronounced facial markings. Their collar is also pinker and much more distinct.

Boreal Ringneck Parakeet (P.k. borealis)

The plumage on the Boreal Ringneck Parakeet (P.k. borealis) is green without any yellow. Males exhibit a blue suffusion behind the ears, and the bills are bigger and all red.

Selective Breeding for Color Mutations

Bird fanciers have bred the Ringneck Parakeet in a large color range in aviaries so that established color mutations are available in yellow, sky blue, grey, olive, pure white and the especially spectacular violet coloration.

Only males of any coloration, natural or mutated, show the distinctive neck ring, which does not appear until the bird is at least 3 years of age. Sexing a Ringneck Parakeet before that age is therefore difficult.

Chapter 2 - Ringneck Parakeets as Pets

It's a common misconception among people who have never kept birds as pets that acquiring one is as simple as running down to the pet store, buying a bird and getting a cage. Nothing could be farther from the truth, especially with a long-lived, gregarious and intelligent species like the Ringneck Parakeet.

It is important to note that both cocks and hens are equally friendly, gregarious and affectionate. It makes no difference which gender you purchase. It is purely a matter of personal preference.

Although you will pay more, it is highly advisable to buy your bird from a breeder at an aviary. Not only should you be assured of getting a healthy pet, but you will be able to talk with the breeder.

It's important to learn from someone with experience how to acclimate your Ringneck to its new home, and the best ways to satisfy the animal's long-term needs.

The major advantage of buying from a breeder is that the birds will, in almost all cases, have been hand raised. They will be completely socialized and accustomed to interaction with humans. This means that from the beginning, you will be able to comfortably handle your new companion, and there will be a greatly reduced risk of accidents or escapes.

What to Know Before Buying a Ringneck Parakeet

Ringneck Parakeets need just as much, or more, interaction as any other kind of companion animal. They adjust very well to family life because they are alert and engaged. These birds crave a stimulating environment with lots to watch and learn. Don't ever make the mistake of isolating a parakeet in some little used corner of the house.

You may be surprised to find out that your bird will exhibit emotions very akin to your own. Parakeets can get deeply lonely, a state they often convey by screeching or plucking their own feathers. As bright creatures in need of sensory input and entertainment, they're also subject to boredom and frustration.

A well-socialized Ringneck Parakeet that is handled routinely and gets lots of human interaction is a docile, friendly companion.

A bird that is obviously annoyed and grumpy, nipping at your fingers and being hostile in general, is not getting what it needs in terms of company, socialization, living space and simple pleasure in life.

Parakeets are easily tamed but they need to be handled daily to stay tame. In adopting one, you are making a commitment to a living creature with a lifespan that can easily extend to 20 years or more. This is one reason why an elderly person might not be the best candidate to own a Ringneck. What will happen to the bird if its human companion dies first?

No companion animal is ever thrilled when its human decides to go on vacation. It's certainly easier to board your dog or to get someone to come in and feed the cat than it is to arrange vacation care for a pet bird.

In the best of all possible cases, someone in your life will know the parakeet and be able to take over in the short-term, but you may find yourself out the price of a professional pet sitter.

There are people who hire out to take care of all kinds of companion animals while their owners are away. Your vet can likely help you locate someone competent and responsible, but you still have to open your home to a stranger and entrust your bird to their care – for a price.

Also, with a Ringneck Parakeet in your life, there will be noise. Even if the parakeet never learns to talk, your bird will make a full range of sounds from chirps and trills, to outright screeches if the occasion warrants.

They love music, and will happily sing along to whatever is playing. You have to be prepared for the noise the parakeet is going to make just being what he is — a bird.

Any time you bring a companion animal into your life, you should seriously consider your ability to care for the creature.

Many people make the mistake of thinking birds are "easy." All you do is just clean the cage and give them some bird seed, right? Wrong.

Before you even think about adopting a Ringneck Parakeet you should learn everything you can about the animal, talking to people who live with them, watching videos online, and at the very least "lurking" in bird discussion forums where you can read first-person experiences.

Be able to answer, honestly, some very important questions:

- Am I prepared for the long-term commitment required to keep a bird that may live 20 years or more?

- Can I realistically provide a safe and appropriate environment for this bird, especially in terms of space?

- Can I allow this bird to be out of its cage every day to get the exercise it needs, even understanding that's going to mean some mess in my life?

- Will the other people in my life, including the neighbors, accept the natural sounds this bird makes?

- Am I willing to accept that even though this bird is in theory for my son or daughter, I have to be an active and responsible part of its care? And that in time, I may become the sole owner of the bird?

It is simply not fair to bring a living creature into your home unless you are planning to give it everything it needs to enjoy a good and healthy life in captivity. Birds are not "easy" pets in the sense of being effortless and requiring no work.

They are "easy" in that when they are well cared for, they are a positive and intriguing addition to your life, and will be long-term affectionate and loyal companions.

Yes, you'll be picking bird seed up off the floor pretty much every day. Most people, however, think that's well worth the genuine joy and excitement with which their Ringneck greets them for no other reason than that they've just walked in the room!

Human Health Considerations

In this book we cover some of the common health issues experienced by Ringneck Parakeeets and some of the zoonotic diseases i.e. a disease that can be transmitted from an animal to a human being. We have also touched on the issue of allergies that can be caused by companion birds such as people being allergic to the dander. Before making the decision to bring a companion bird into your life, we strongly recommend that you take advice from your doctor and veterinarian so that you have a full understanding of any risks to your own health.

Where to Buy Ringneck Parakeets in the US and UK

The following is provided as a partial list of aviaries only, and is not intended as a comprehensive source, nor does the author specifically endorse any of these facilities.

Aviaries in the U.S.

Abby's Bird Corner

AbbysBirdCorner.weebly.com

Best Birds Aviary (Florida) – http://thebestbird.com

Cherry Blossom Aviary and Parrots Nest (Kentucky)

http://theparrotsnest.webs.com/

Corbett Birds (Illinois) - CorbettBirds.com

Dandy Birds (Virginia) - DandAviary.weebly.com

EMR Exotic Bird Breeder (California)

EMRExoticBirdBreeder.com

Feathered Companions

443-359-4029

Irena's Aviary (Alabama)

205 429 4367

Parrotville Bird Shop (Ohio)

ParrotVille.com

S&L Exotic Feathers (Massachusetts) 508-509-7599

Singing Wings Aviary (Arkansas)

Singing-Wings-Aviary.com

The Bird Lady (Texas)

956-309-0750

Aviaries in the UK

West Lynn Aviary

King's Lynn, Norfolk

http://west-lynn-aviary.webs.com/

Facebook; Lynn Aviary

Riverside Aviaries

Mill lane, Titchfield, Hampshire

Tel: 01329 846521

www.riversideaviaries.co.uk/birds.htm#ringnecks

Edinburgh Breeder of hand reared

African Greys, Macaws, Senegals, Pionus, Ringneck

Cockatiels, Conures and Rosa Bourkes

Tel: 0131 553 6067

DG & E Bennett (Upper Swansea Valley) Breeders of mutation Indian Ringnecks.

Tel: 01639 841432

London Birds (Sue Turner/Diana Malin)

Babies for sale: Ringnecks, Rosellas, Cockatiels, Kakarikis, Budgerigars.

Email: halliwick@planet-save.com

Wattle Grove Aviaries, Just outside Liverpool

www.wattlegroveaviaries.weebly.com/indian-ringneck-parrot.html

West Midlands

Email: debandbatch@msn.com
debandbatch@blueyonder.co.uk

Mue.B@btinternet.com

www.bestofbreeds.co.uk

marypayne@tinyworld.co.uk

K & M Barnes - parrot/parakeet breeders, 15+ year's experience. Hand-reared cuddly babies available all year, from cockatiels to conures, poicephalus, A/Greys & Amazons. Norfolk Tel: 01953-455444

Bringing Your New Ringneck Parakeet Home

The degree to which you are able to handle your parakeet from the beginning depends on how the bird was raised.

If it is the product of an aviary that engages in hand-raising techniques, the Ringneck will immediately be receptive to hopping up on your finger and having a look around. He'll be curious, playful and confident, which is one of the major reasons to buy a bird from a breeder rather than a pet store.

If he is obviously agitated and frightened, a period of adjustment and a patient program of taming lie ahead of you.

Calling Your Bird's Bluff

Depending on the age of your Ringneck Parakeet, you may have to deal with an adolescent behavior called "bluffing," which is very trying at best.

The key word to concentrate on here is "adolescent." If you bring a "teenager" home, even one with feathers, you still have to deal with the fallout of hormones on attitude.

Young birds going through bluffing will engage in hissing, biting, nipping, lunging and just overall resistance to any kind of interaction. The negative behaviors can last for 4 months to a year.

It's a mistake to completely confine a bluffing bird or to stop attempts at socialization and handling. You'll probably get nipped, but just tough it out, and above all, don't scream at the bird.

Ringneck Parakeets don't actually perceive loud vocalizations as a negative. If you scream at your bird, all you'll get is a bird that screams right back!

Also, tough as it is, don't pull away when the bird nips at you. If anything, you need to push into the bite. The point is to show your obstinate little bird that he's not getting one over on you!

The good news is that the Parakeet will get over it all in time. He's just growing up, and, like a good parent, you have to grin and bear it all until he does.

Ringneck Parakeets and Children

Ringneck Parakeets are not especially sensitive to age when it comes to their likes and dislikes. They bond with some people and don't like others, irrespective of age and gender.

As long as children are quiet and kind to the bird, they stand an equal chance of getting along well with the creature. However, parakeets do not like to be grabbed or startled.

It is imperative that a child be taught how to properly interact and care for a companion bird.

Once a parakeet takes a dislike to someone, it's pretty much impossible to get these obstinate little birds to change their minds.

Ringneck Parakeets and Other Pets

Obviously for the comfort level of your parakeet, the bird needs to be kept well away from other pets that would cause it anxiety, such as cats and dogs. But what many people do not realize is that parakeets can be quite overtly aggressive to other animals.

Parakeets tend to bond strongly with one human and can display outright jealousy in the presence of other animals. This can be expressed loudly and vocally, with outright attacks if the bird is able to do so, and even by flinging items at the offending pet.

A loose parakeet is quite capable of torturing a small dog with "flybys" and other harassing behavior. Any animal that is sensitive to loud noises, like rabbits, will not enjoy being around a Ringneck when it is screeching and angry.

What About Wing Clipping?

If you are completely new to owning a companion bird and this is your first parakeet, you may well receive advice about having the bird's wings clipped.

Customarily this has been a precaution against accidents that occur when the bird becomes startled and gets away from a nervous, new owner.

Young birds indoors have a tendency to fly into windows and mirrors — really anything that gets in their way — and they can injure themselves seriously.

The traditional method of handling this problem has been to clip back the bird's flight feathers, but that practice is highly controversial and really no longer in favor for a number of good reasons.

First and foremost, clipping a bird's wings is an unnatural

act akin to clipping a barking dog's vocal chords or de-clawing a cat. Birds are meant to fly, and if they cannot, there can be serious consequences.

Although theoretically done in the name of protecting the bird, wing clipping is really a matter of convenience for the owner. Yes, it's more trouble to make sure the windows and doors are closed, or that netting is put up to prevent dangerous collisions, but you have adopted a bird.

When a young bird's flight feathers are clipped, the animal will never become good at flying for the simple reason that it cannot develop its chest muscles appropriately.

Even if the flight feathers are allowed to grow back (and this may take three years), the parakeet will never be efficient and capable in flight.

Also, realize that in clipping the feathers, you've compromised the bird's primary means of keeping itself safe — the ability to escape.

Unless the parakeet can fly, it can't get away from threats like dogs and cat. Not to mention the fact that, if done inappropriately, clipping the wings can injure the bird so severely it will bleed to death.

Many parakeets begin to pluck their own feathers after their wings are clipped, likely as a sign of frustration that they cannot follow their natural instincts.

This dissatisfaction can also play out with episodes of aggression and other negative behaviors.

As part of the process of getting to know your Ringneck Parakeet, you have to learn to safely handle the bird, including the times that it is out of the cage.

While wing clipping has long been a control measure with companion birds, it presents a true moral dilemma for bird owners and should be avoided.

Introducing a Second Bird to the Household

If you already own a Ringneck Parakeet and have decided to get a second bird, it is absolutely imperative that the new parakeet has a clean bill of health.

You may have purchased your first bird from a pet store, but for a second bird, it's best to go to an aviary with a reputation for raising healthy animals.

Bird diseases and parasites are highly contagious. Introducing a second bird with a health problem could be fatal for both parakeets.

The best practice is to have a new bird evaluated by a veterinarian before bringing it into an environment with an existing pet Ringneck.

It is common for breeders to offer some kind of health guarantee as well as vet certification of that fact. The extra money you will pay is well worth the peace of mind these assurances convey.

Even with all these precautions, keep the new bird in a separate room for at least two weeks to observe the animal and to make sure no signs of disease surface. During this period, thoroughly wash your hands after handling either bird and before touching the other.

Clean the new bird's cage last after working with your original Ringneck. You, too, can be an agent of disease transmission, so it's imperative that you take extra care until the birds are ready to be introduced to one another and to share a single habitat.

Do not integrate the two birds until you are sure the new parakeet is eating and drinking regularly and is passing firm stools. There should be no discharge around the eyes or nose, and the feathers should be smooth and lying flat.

When you are sure the new bird is healthy, place the two cages side by side for a few days. At the point at which the birds are happily "talking" or touching bills through the bars, you are ready to integrate their environment.

Obviously, you only want to house a cock and a hen together if you are planning to breed the animals. Otherwise, it is rare for parakeets to fight once they have had an opportunity to check each other out. These birds tend to be just as companionable with one another as they are with their humans. You should however bear in mind that there are no guarantees that your Ringneck Parakeets will get on. If this happens, are you happy to house both birds separately? If you would not be prepared to do this or would not have the space to do this, it would be better not to get a second bird.

Time Away from Your Parrot

All pet owners face one common concern: What happens when it is time to go on vacation? Many people travel with their pets, but the fact is pets cannot always go with their families. What will you do with your bird when you have to go away from home – on vacation or out of town for business or for a funeral, for example?

Consider who will watch your bird before the need ever arises. You have several options. Perhaps a friend or a family member, who has been around your bird and feels comfortable, can bring him home to care for him.

Pet sitters are also a popular option, especially in the United States where pet sitting businesses must be licensed and insured to operate. A pet sitter generally comes to your home to visit your pet – to ensure he has food, water, and time out to exercise. Pet sitters typically charge per visit, and you can schedule several visits each day.

Is a pet sitter a viable option for your bird? That depends. How long will you be gone? Can you afford to have the pet sitter come several times each day to ensure your bird will get time out of his cage? Be sure, if you look for a pet sitter, to find someone who has experience caring for birds or who is willing to take the time to learn about parakeets and their care.

Before you hire a pet sitter or agree to a visiting schedule, the pet sitter will generally come to your home for an initial consultation. During that meeting, you will chat with the pet sitter about your bird, his schedule, his diet and how often he requires a visit each day. But, more importantly, the meeting will allow your bird and the pet sitter to meet and to become comfortable around each other. Some pet sitters charge for this initial meeting but many do not.

You can find pet sitters in the United States through the National Association of Pet Sitters (www.petsitters.org) and Pet Sitters International (www.petsit.com).

A comprehensive list of pet sitters in the United Kingdom can be found through the National Association of Registered Pet Sitters (www.dogsit.com) and yes, they look after more than dogs!

Make sure that your pet sitter is insured and fully referenced as they will have access to you home and your pet. You should also contact your home insurance providers to confirm your cover is not affected by having a pet sitter stay at your home.

If you do not like the idea of a pet sitter, consider contacting your local parrot or large bird rescue. Some rescue organizations offer boarding and pet sitting services while others may just be able to provide you with recommendations of sitters.

The Parrot Society of the UK – or local bird groups – may also have members who offer to pet sit parakeets while their owners are on vacation.

If you do the footwork – asking friends, investigating pet sitters, and talking with local bird groups – you should have little trouble finding a knowledgeable person to watch your bird for you.

Coming Home Again

How will your parrot react when you return home, especially if you have been gone a considerable period? Well, birds are like people, so do not be surprised if your beloved friend is angry with you for having left him. And, like people, he will need time to shed that anger.

Be gentle with your parrot, talking to him and treating him like normal, so he can become reassured that everything is okay. Do not become overly aggressive with him or push him to adjust to his normal life. Doing so could backfire, and your bird may need even more time to get back to normal.

Pros and Cons of Owning a Ringneck Parakeet

As with most companion animals, the "pros" and "cons" of owning a Ringneck Parakeet are interchangeable in many cases depending on the attitude of the prospective "owner."

The most often cited negatives by people who find out they don't like keeping a bird are the noise and the mess. Ringneck Parakeets are not as loud as some companion species, but they're hardly quiet either.

The cage will require daily maintenance. They do scatter their food, and when they free fly . . . well, the bird is hardly going to go back to his cage just to do his "business".

The fact that Ringneck Parakeets are highly social and require a great deal of interaction is both a positive and a negative.

Many people who adopt a Ringneck Parakeet discover,

the simple reason that the first parakeet is lonely and unhappy. While having a friend will certainly relieve the first Ringneck's unhappiness, it doubtless increases the required maintenance involved and as already mentioned, there is no guarantee that the two birds will bond.

The major advantage of keeping a parakeet lies in sharing your life with an intelligent species capable of understanding and amassing language and learning intricate behaviors. Parakeets experience definite, identifiable emotions. They are loving and incredibly loyal.

Ringneck Parakeets are also long lived, some surviving more than 20 years. Again, this can be both a positive and a negative. Adopting one of these birds represents a real commitment, and one that should not be taken up lightly.

Your best safeguard against making a bad decision that will affect your life and that of the parakeet is to learn everything you can before you proceed. Keeping a bird is not like having a dog or cat, or a goldfish in a bowl.

A parakeet is not a passive non-entity that can just be stuck in a cage with some food and water. They are interested and interesting creatures that will depend on you for their emotional and physical stability.

Never buy a Ringneck Parakeet on impulse!

If, however, you learn everything you can and your impulse is still to buy? You're about to welcome an absolutely remarkable animal into your life, one that will bring you years of joyful friendship.

Projected Costs

A healthy Ringneck Parakeet from a reputable breeder - $150 - $225 (£97.50 - £146.25)

These prices can be higher for a rare color and may be $350 (£227.50) or more.

Note that Ringneck Parakeets can be purchased from pet stores including "big box" retail outlets for less, sometimes under $50 (£32.50), but if you are planning to breed your birds, this is likely not your best option.

Initial Set-Up

Cage - $250 (£162.50)

Ladders and Swings - $5 to $15 (£3.25 to £9.75) each

Perches $5 to $15 (£3.25 to £9.75) each

Toys $4 to $15 (£2.60 to £9.75) each

Mixed daily commercial feed

2.5 lbs. (1.13 kg.) - $10 (£6.50)

20 lbs. (9.07 kg.) - $50 (£32.50)

Treats

1 to 5 lbs. (0.45 kg. to 2.27 kg.) - $6 to $25 (£3.90 to £16.25)

Multi-Vitamins

4 oz. (4.16 fl. oz. UK) bottle - $15 (£9.75)

3.5 oz. (99.2 g) of pellets - $10 (£6.50)

Cuttlebone $1 (£0.65)

Mineral Block

Small blocks $2 (£1.30)

Large blocks $4 (£2.60)

Lava Stone

2.5 inches x 2.5 inches x 1.25 inches (6.35 centimeters x 6.35 centimeters x 3.18 centimeters)

$5 (£3.25)

Feeder cups

$2 (£1.30)

Feeders with scatter guards

$10 to $15 (£6.50 - £9.75)

Waterer

$2 to $15 (£1.30 to £9.75)

Bath

$6 to $10 (£3.90 to £6.50)

Carrier

$60 to $120 (£39 to £78)

To fully outfit a brand new Ringneck Parakeet habitat, the minimum budget would be $400 (£260).

Breeding Supplies

Nesting Box

$5 to $10 (£3.25 - £6.50)

Plastic pipette / syringe / eye dropper

$1 (£0.65) each

Heat lamp with thermostat

$35 to $50 (£22.75 to £32.50)

Replacement bulbs

$10 to $15 (£6.50 to £9.75) each

Digital thermometer

$7 to $10 (£4.55 to £6.50)

Hand feeding formula

18 oz. (0.51 kgs) g sells for $10 (£6.50)

Chapter 3 - Daily Care

There is a great deal more to having a pet bird than buying a cage and putting the parakeet inside. If that is your idea of keeping a companion bird, a parakeet is not the pet for you.

You also have to be realistic about the amount of room the bird will need in your home. Remember that as an adult, your parakeet will be almost 16 inches (40.6 centimeters) in length.

If you put the bird in a cage that's too small, it will suffer broken tail feathers and severe emotional distress.

Look at your available space, and make sure you have enough room for the kind of home your bird will need to be comfortable and healthy.

Remember that long, wide cages are better than tall, narrow ones and plan accordingly.

If you're ready to proceed, you can start making out your shopping list.

Shopping for Your Ringneck Parakeet

In the beginning, your parakeet will need a number of supplies for his new home. Your initial purchases should include all of the following items :

Cage

Parakeets are active and playful birds and therefore they require a roomy cage. Those labeled "flight cage" or "cockatiel" are often the best choice.

Size is not the only consideration. Make certain the bars are not wide enough for the bird to stick his head through. He will panic and injure or kill himself.

The bars should be spaced at a width not greater than 0.5 inches (1.27 centimeters).

The minimum recommended cage size is:

36 inches long x 24 inches deep x 48 inches high (91.4 centimeters x 61 centimeters x 122 centimeters)

If possible, get a cage with horizontal bars on the side to help the bird climb. The best materials are stainless steel and BPA free hard plastics.

While antique or wooden cages may have an appealing aesthetic look, they are easily damaged and can be a breeding ground for harmful bacteria.

Always get the largest cage you can afford. Bigger is always better with a Ringneck Parakeet enclosure.

Square or rectangular cages are the best option. You may like the look of a round cage, but your bird will enjoy having a corner to "scrunch" into.

Also, round cages are not as spacious for the bird as they might appear.

As an example of an appropriate enclosure, a cage (on a wheeled stand) measuring 42 inches x 32 inches x 68 inches (107cm x 81.5 centimeters x 173centimeters) with four food cups and two birch wood perches can be purchased online from DrsFosterSmith.com for about $250 (£162.50).

Is Outdoors an Option?

In truth, it's something of a misconception — and conceivably an injustice — to refer to a Ringneck Parakeet as a "cage" bird. All birds, especially companion birds, need room to fly and to experience the world around them.

Many people who keep companion birds maintain larger home enclosures in their yards so their pets can have greater freedom with proper security and supervision. Technically these enclosures are referred to as aviaries and can be of any size and shape you can afford. The same stipulations for materials and safety apply.

If you are a "do it yourself" type, there are many plans available online, or you can consult with a contractor to get an idea of the cost involved.

Note: Always transfer your parakeet from home to aviary in a secure travel crate, and only release the bird in the aviary when you are certain there is no chance of escape.

Once you've determined the enclosure or enclosures your bird will use, it's time to get his "furniture".

Ladders and Swings

Swings and ladders both encourage natural climbing and perching activity in caged parakeets.

Expect to pay $5 to $15 (£3.25 to £9.75) each depending on the size and complexity of the individual piece.

Perches in a Variety of Sizes

The rule of thumb is the larger your cage, the more perches you will want to provide for your bird.

Remember, parakeets are an observant species. They'll enjoy having numerous vantage points in their cage, and moving from one perch to another is good exercise for the bird. Simple perches cost under $5 (£3.25) while more elaborate pieces may cost as much as $15 (£9.75).

Toys

Parakeets love any kind of "shredding" toy. These birds can be highly destructive chewers. You need to be aware of this when they're out of their cage, too!

You'll go through more toys than you realize, but parakeets are much happier when they're "working" on something.

Expect to pay $4 to $15 (£2.60 to £9.75) depending on the complexity of the toy.

Treats

Although it's perfectly acceptable and even healthy to give your parakeet fresh fruits and vegetables, many bird owners opt for freeze-dried fruit and vegetable treats due to ease of storage.

Most are purchased in bulk from 1 to 5 lbs. (0.45 kg. to 2.27 kg.) in a price range of $6 to $25 (£3.90 to £16.25).

Seed / Pellet Food

Your parakeet will do best on a diet of seed and pellets with fresh fruits and vegetables mixed in. Mixed commercial feeds appropriate for daily use are available in varying bag sizes.

An average price for 2.5 lbs. (1.13 kg) is $10 (£6.50) with 20 lbs. (9.07 kg) retailing for $50 (£32.50).

Vitamins

Vitamins for parakeets come in both pellet and liquid forms. Arguably a bird on a well-balanced diet does not require supplementation, but the vitamins are a good precaution.

A 4 oz. (4.16 fl. oz. UK) bottle of a multi-vitamin retails for $15 (£9.75) with 3.5 oz. (99.2 g) of pellets selling for approximately $10 (£6.50).

Always dispense according to the instructions on the label.

Cuttlebone

A cuttlebone is the shell of the Cuttlefish, a cephalopod that is something like a small squid. Cuttlebones are widely harvested as jaw exercise toys and supplements for birds.

If you've never seen a cuttlebone, it's a lightweight, chalky, oblong object made mostly of calcium. The texture is grainy, like pumice, which also makes it useful in keeping the bird's beak worn down.

Most cuttlebones sell for about $1 (£0.65).

Mineral Block

Like cuttlebones, mineral blocks provide parakeets with a

source of calcium and other minerals while encouraging natural chewing and wearing down of the beak.

Working on the block keeps the bird entertained, especially if you get a product that has a hidden treat on the inside.

Parakeets have good memories. They will recognize a fresh block for what it is, and set about getting at the treat immediately.

Small mineral blocks retail for around $2 (£1.30), with larger sizes going for $4 (£2.60).

Lava Stone

Parakeets especially enjoy lava stones for beak cleaning, and in the process, more beak trimming is accomplished.

Stones vary in size. Expect to pay about $5 (£3.25) for a one measuring 2.5 inches x 2.5 inches x 1.25 inches (6.35 centimeters x 6.35 centimeters x 3.18 centimeters).

Food and Water Dishes

Simple cups that hang on the side of the cage to hold food and water are priced as low as $2 (£1.30). These come in both plastic and stainless steel options. Ensure any plastic items are BPA and non-toxic.

Variations on this theme are "no mess" feeders, which encase the tray in a clear box, or feature some kind of "scatter guard" mechanism.

Expect to pay $10 to $15 (£6.50 to £9.75) for these more elaborate units.

Waterers range from around $2 to $15 (£1.30 to £9.75) depending on size and drinking mechanism.

For the most part, inverted bottles that dispense the water according to the pull of gravity are the most popular. Some allow the water to collect in a tray, others have a "lixit" feeding device tip outfitted with a ball bearing.

Bath

Parakeets love to bathe and will happily use a small "tub" affixed to the side of their cage.

These units are inexpensive and retail for $6 to $10 (£3.90 to £6.50).

As a hint, don't fill the bath too full. In the wild, parakeets bathe in wet grass, not puddles, so they aren't huge fans of deep water, plus they'll just make a bigger mess with more bath water.

Invest in a Carrier

You will also want to invest in a carrier if you ever have to transport your bird to the vet, secure it during a change in residence, or need to temporarily confine the parakeet for any reason. An important example would be when you're cleaning his main cage.

Carriers are also described as "travel cages" and retail for $60 to $120 (£39 to £78).

Arranging Your Ringneck Parakeet's Home

Once all of your supplies are in place, you'll be arranging your parakeet's home not only to encourage movement and give the bird a stimulating environment, but also to minimize contamination of food and water sources and to facilitate cage cleaning.

Always include, as a minimum, two perches in the cage that are roughly three-quarters of an inch (1.91 centimeters) in diameter. I recommend you err on the side of "more is better" without cluttering up the cage.

Food and water dishes should hang from the side of the cage and position all perches and toys well away from them to prevent contamination from droppings.

You can certainly purchase manufactured perches, but remember that Ringneck Parakeets love to chew.

If you select fresh branches from fruit trees, oaks, or maple, the bird will be more entertained by the irregular shape and you'll save a little money.

Also, different densities of wood help to keep the parakeet's beak and nails naturally well-trimmed.

When you use fresh perches, remove them at the first sign of drying and put new ones in place. This is an excellent way to provide variety for your parakeet.

Never use perches that are covered in sandpaper. They will irritate the parakeet's feet and create the potential for infection.

Considering Temperature and Ventilation

Cage placement is extremely important. You're looking for the correct balance of light and ventilation but don't subject the parakeet to a draft.

Stay away from glass doors and windows. Directly exposing the bird to the sun makes temperature regulation difficult.

Parakeets do best during the day at temperatures of 60 F to 70 F / 15.6 C - 21.1 C, and should never be allowed to experience less than 40 F / 4.4 C at night. Cover the cage at night to give the bird privacy and to keep it warmer.

If the bird's feathers are fluffed out for long periods of time, the parakeet is probably cold. If it is holding its wings away from its body and panting, the bird is overheated.

Choose a High Location for the Cage

Parakeets feed on the ground in the wild and are naturally programmed to be on the lookout for danger at that level. If the cage is placed too low, the bird will be subjected to a constant state of vigilance, which is highly stressful.

Also, the cage should be high enough that neither the family cat nor dog will be able to pester the bird.

The best cage placement is the one which makes the parakeet feel most secure. Observe the bird's behavior for clues about how he feels about the location of his cage.

Cage Placement Affects Socialization

It's important to remember that you and your family are the parakeet's "flock." Place the cage against one wall so the bird feels safer, but don't put it in any out of the way area like a bedroom or hallway.

Parakeets like to be able to see activity and to feel that they are part of the family. This will help the bird to stay friendly and socialized, intellectually engaged, and will facilitate the acquisition of language if that is one of your hopes for your pet.

Clean the Parakeet's Cage Daily

Each day you will want to clean your bird's food and water bowls. Lay fresh newspaper (or some similar material) down on the bottom of the cage.

Never make the mistake of using cat litter in the bottom of a parakeet's cage. The bird will eat the litter, which can be fatal.

On a weekly basis, wash and disinfect the cage with warm, soapy water. This includes perches and all of the bird's toys. Make sure everything is nice and dry before you return the parakeet to its cage.

On a monthly basis, dismantle the cage and take it outside or put it in the tub for a thorough wash down.

Opt for natural disinfectants like vinegar for washing and baking soda for scrubbing. Avoid household chemicals, many of which are deadly to your pet.

Whenever cleaning, make sure all cleaning residue is removed from the cage and its components, and that everything has dried out before you put the bird back inside.

Feeding Your Ringneck Parakeet

If you're new to keeping a parakeet, you likely have the preconceived notion that your pet's diet will primarily be bird seed.

Certainly Ringneck Parakeets enjoy seeds, but they will receive better balanced nutrition from pellet foods and fresh fruits and vegetables.

Roughly 60 to 70% of your bird's diet should be from prepared bird pellets, with the remainder coming from fresh foods.

Dark, leafy vegetables are an excellent source of vitamins for parakeets. Also feed it carrots and broccoli. Good fruit choices include: kiwi, melon, apples and pears.

After a couple of hours, take any uneaten foods out of the cage. Don't give your parakeet apple seeds, rhubarb, cherry pits or avocado. All are toxic to your bird.

Note: This list is not comprehensive, and in order to determine whether a specific food is toxic for your parakeet, please check with your breeder or veterinarian. When in doubt, do not give the food to your bird.

Cuttlebones will help to keep the parakeet's beak trimmed, and are a source of necessary calcium.

Except for dispensing fresh foods at irregular intervals, keep your parakeet's feeder filled at all times. Clean the feeder and waterer daily to reduce the risk of bacterial infection.

Always provide your Ringneck Parakeet with fresh, chlorine-free water. Bath water should also be de-chlorinated.

Handling Your Parakeet

When a parakeet is new to a household, it's important to let the bird become accustomed to its surroundings. Your pet is an intelligent and observant creature that will watch what's going on around him and take in information about you and your routines.

Don't underestimate the power of such a tiny creature to be a bit of a bully, especially if the bird is an adolescent and exhibiting hormonally-induced "bluffing" behavior. It's a mistake to be afraid of your bird, or to let the parakeet think you're afraid of him.

In the end, your fear only leads to unhappiness for both of you, and serious neglect for the bird. Especially if aggression is coming from "bluffing," the negative behaviors resolve in just a few months. Ostracizing your parakeet for simply going through puberty will punish the bird for life for something he can't help!

Remember simple rules for getting your Ringneck Parakeet used to being handled.

- Birds do not like quick movements or loud noises.

- Move slowly and use a soft voice.

- Never shake the cage.

- Allow the bird time out of the cage to free fly.

- Give the bird the security of a routine.

- Let your parakeet have "down time."

The first "training" lesson is simply establishing that you are a trustworthy companion for the parakeet.

Hold your finger out in front of your bird, talking to it softly. Be patient. After a few days the parakeet will start to nudge at your finger, and eventually it will hop up and perch.

Please note that Ringneck Parakeets that have been hand raised in an aviary are tamer, and will generally begin to interact with their new humans immediately upon arriving in a new home.

Never, under any circumstances, grab the bird or hold it tightly enough to make it feel it's being squeezed. You will only terrify the poor creature, and erode the trust you've worked hard to establish.

To pick up your pet, put your palm lightly on your bird's back and gently wrap your fingers around the bird with your thumb and forefinger on either side of its head.

Especially in the beginning of the relationship, your parakeet may nip at you with its beak, but the bites aren't painful or serious. Don't overreact. Remain calm with the bird at all times, and show your pet that you are a gentle and attentive caregiver.

Teaching Your Ringneck Parakeet to Talk

Ringneck Parakeets have the ability to amass working vocabularies of around 250 words. The more interactive you are with your parakeet, including simply talking to it as you go about your daily routine, the more likely it is to learn and to copy your speech.

Is Your Parakeet Actually Communicating?

It's a matter of some debate as to whether or not the bird really understands what it's saying. Parakeet owners, however, are fairly universal in their agreement that their pets give the right answers and sometimes even ask the right questions!

But more importantly, even non-speaking parakeets respond correctly, indicating their ability to learn words whether they use them or not. When Ringneck Parakeets do begin to talk, they mimic intonation pronunciation and accents.

Male parakeets are more likely to learn to speak than females, but females can be taught to whistle, and appear to enjoy doing so.

Repetition is the Key

When your parakeet does start to talk, respond as if the bird were a child. Name things for it, and give it verbal cues. If, for instance, you offer the bird a treat and it takes the goodie, cue the parakeet with the phrase, "Thank you!"

Always be consistent with the language you use, since the bird's first efforts will be merely repetition. However, parakeets are smart, and when they see that the words they are using elicit desired responses, they naturally expand what they're doing to get more of what they want, either your time and attention, or another treat!

Be Aware of Background Noise

Don't be at all surprised if your clever Ringneck suddenly calls the dog, tells your son to, "Pick up your socks!" or comes out with a line from your favorite TV show.

Anything verbal that is going on in the background of your life is fair game for your parakeet's learning curve.

Is it possible that your bird may learn to say something you wish he hadn't? Yes, having a Ringneck in the house can be a little like raising a precocious toddler with feathers.

Especially if you have a bird that is taking well to talking and picking up words fast, so be careful what you say!

Since repetition is the key to teaching a parakeet to talk, anything you say over and over again qualifies as a "lesson", including your favorite swear words.

For more information on teaching your Ringneck Parakeet to talk, see this informative video, "How to teach a bird to talk, a step by step tutorial"

http://www.youtube.com/watch?v=o3oE_8EJa-E

Feather Plucking - A Sure Sign of Unhappiness

Birds may not communicate with our kind of language (even if they do learn to talk), but they send plenty of clear signals on their own.

If your parakeet starts plucking its own feathers out, the bird is bored, lonely or sick.

If there are two birds housed in the same cage, feather loss may also be due to aggression from the other birds.

Pay careful attention for any signs of discord, and separate the birds if one is trying to hurt the other.

If you have to be gone several hours a day, consider keeping a pair of parakeets rather than a lone bird. These are highly social creatures. They need friendship.

Some people believe that giving the bird a mirror to create the illusion of companionship is sufficient, but while a mirror helps, it is not a total solution.

To learn more about Ringneck Parakeet health, see Chapter Four.

Time to Free Fly

Do not think that you will keep a parakeet happy and healthy by just letting it sit in a cage all day. Time to free fly, in a safe, secure room is a very important part of your bird's life.

Provide a shallow bath outside the cage filled with clean, lukewarm water. Be sure to lay down newspapers to catch the mess when your parakeet splashes and has a good time in its "pool".

Your pet will quickly develop a routine of flying in and out of its cage, perhaps perching on a plant with a good view of the outside through a nearby window, taking a dip in its bath, or playing with other toys you provide. This is, for the bird, the most "natural" part of its existence.

You can potentially direct your bird's movements and maybe control the amount of droppings that fall out of the cage during free time by providing your Ringneck Parakeet with a couple of playgrounds outside his cage.

These units are generally constructed as edged trays, with built in perches, swings, bells and ladders.

Think of them as "landing stations" in your bird safe room. The parts break down for easy washing.

A typical product measures 14.5 inches x 12.5 inches x 9.25 inches / 36.8 centimeters x 31.7 centimeters x 23.5 centimeters and includes a "jungle gym" type arrangement of toys and perches. Expect to pay about $20 (£13) per playground.

Nap Time and Sleeping

It's normal for Ringneck Parakeets to take naps during the day. You can encourage this practice at a given hour by dimming the lights and making the room quiet.

At night, your bird will sleep 10 to 12 hours. Not all bird owners cover the cage at night, but this is a perfect way to ensure the parakeet has a good dark environment and a sense of privacy.

Quick Facts: Common Parakeet Behaviors

While your Ringneck Parakeet will certainly have a distinct personality all its own, there are a number of behaviors that are common to all parakeets:

- Dancing at the cage door.

Your bird is saying, very plainly, "How about letting me out of here?" The more your parakeet becomes accustomed to time outside the cage, the more it will ask, in this adorable way, to get out and play.

Ringneck Parakeets are very smart. Don't be surprised when your pet learns your schedule and starts expecting play time according to the clock.

Attempts to change what your bird sees as his daily routine may well be greeted with squawking protests.

- "Praying" with head tipped forward.

This is a blatant request for attention. Parakeets love to have their little heads scratched. They're asking you to do what they'd ask another bird to do for them, a little friendly preening.

Birds especially like to have their heads scratched because this is an area they can't reach by themselves.

- Head tucking and bobbing.

It's perfectly normal for a parakeet to sleep with its head tucked into its fluffed-up back feathers. To you it may look like the most uncomfortable position in the world, but you're not a bird!

By the same token, Ringneck Parakeets often bob their heads as if they're listening to some internal music we can't hear. This may happen during feeding, or as part of mating dances.

- Regurgitation.

Sometimes head bobbing leads to an episode of regurgitation. Hard as this may be to understand, there is no more intense sign of affection from a parakeet.

Regurgitation is how parakeets feed their babies and feed one another. It may be a little gross, but it's also — in bird speak — a huge compliment.

Please note however, if the bird vomits on its chest, and the material is sticking to its face and feathers and obviously annoying the parakeet, your pet needs veterinary attention.

- Flaring of the wings as the bird backs into a corner.

This territorial movement signals that the bird is frightened or even angry. His message is, "Stay back!" Rather than agitate the parakeet more, just leave it alone if at all possible until it calms down.

- Shaking and fluffing out the feathers.

There are several potential interpretations for this behavior. It may signal that the bird is getting ready to do something, or that the parakeet is sleepy and ready to go to "bed". If a parakeet just sits with its feathers fluffed out, the bird is cold.

- Wing flapping.

Often, parakeets will sit on their perches and furiously flap their wings. There is no need for alarm. The bird is simply exercising and blowing off some steam. No matter how large the cage or aviary, birds — just to be birds — need to feel their wings moving.

They may also flap their wings to loosen the feathers if they're molting. This will speed up the process of new feathers growing in.

- Sneezing and yawning.

Don't be concerned if your bird sneezes occasionally. This does not necessarily signal illness, just a need to clear the nasal passages.

Like humans, parakeets sneeze and yawn and their yawns are as contagious as ours. If you have two birds in a cage and one gets sleepy and starts yawning, the other will get equally "droopy" right on cue.

- Slamming toys around the cage.

Parakeets do get bored and frustrated. If a bird starts throwing things around the cage, it could be saying it's sick of being locked up. If, however, it's mating season, the bird could be suffering from a different kind of frustration.

Male birds who are feeling romantic will also prance up and down on their perch and scratch at their faces.

- Doing parakeet "yoga".

People who are new to keeping companion birds are often surprised at just how flexible these creatures can be. The first time you watch your Ringneck Parakeet lift one leg and wing and stretch them both simultaneously, you'll be surprised by the bird's balance and agility. This maneuver is called "mantling".

It's also quite common for a parakeet to rest on one leg, or even to sleep that way.

In addition to these behaviors, expect your parakeet to spend a lot of time grooming its feathers. This is a sign of good health.

Birds like their feathers to be neat and orderly, with no debris, which is why they preen all the time. In fact, if your bird isn't preening, you need to be concerned and watch the parakeet for other signs of ill health.

Should the lack of grooming reach a point where the bird actually looks "ruffled" or disheveled and some of its feathers are missing, the parakeet is definitely sick.

At the same time that this preening is going on, parakeets will scratch. This does not necessarily indicate the presence of parasites like mites or lice. If, however, the bird scratches to the point of bleeding, or gets bald patches, it should be examined by a veterinarian.

If you have two or more parakeets housed together, you will see mutual grooming called "allopreening".

There are many areas of its body a parakeet can't reach, like the top of the head, and friendly or mated pairs help each other out. When two parakeets do this, it's a sure sign of bonding.

Chapter 4 - Health

Like many small animals that are always on the lookout for larger predators, Ringneck Parakeets try to hide the symptoms of illness rather than appear weak and vulnerable to attack.

It's important to keep a close eye on your bird and to spot any signs of sickness or disease as early as possible.

The Signs of a Healthy Bird

Since you should be handling your Ringneck Parakeet daily to keep the bird well socialized, it's easy to observe key health indicators.

- The bird should be sociable, alert and active.

- His nostrils (nares) located on the fleshy area just above the beak (cere) should be clean and free of any sign of discharge.

- The cere itself should not be crusty or peeling.

- The bird's eyes should be round, clear and bright with an interested expression and no sign of crustiness or discharge.

- The ears should not be visible. These small holes are located just behind the eyes toward the back of the head. They are covered by a layer of fine feathers and should be hidden from sight unless the parakeet is wet from bathing.

- The vent (the area under the tail feathers) should be dry and clean.

- The feathers should be well-groomed, appearing shiny and tight and lying smoothly in place.

- The beak, legs and feet should all appear normal.

Please note that some parakeets do have deformed feet and legs due to improper hatching, but these birds are quite capable of adapting and can still be great companions.

Healthy, happy parakeets eat and drink throughout the day.

The Signs of an Unhealthy Bird

Some signs that a bird may not be feeling well include:

- Being lethargic. Birds do take naps during the day, and they sleep 10 to 12 hours at night, but a parakeet that sleeps all day is not feeling well.

- Sitting on the bottom of the cage. Perching takes energy. A bird that is sitting on the bottom of the cage may feel too weak to perch.

- Fluffed out feathers. Sick parakeets fluff out their feathers to look bigger than they are as a defense mechanism, and to stay warm. If your bird stays fluffed out for extended periods, he could be sick.

- Loose stools or excessive defecation. Stool changes in consistency or color that last for more than a day are always a sign of illness.

- Discharge from the eyes or nose. Both the eyes and nose should always be dry and clear. Any sign of discharge means the parakeet is sick.

- Loss of appetite. If the food level is not dropping according to the bird's regular habits and the parakeet is losing weight, something is wrong.

- Squawking to excess. Otherwise quiet birds that begin to squawk and seem demanding are likely to be in pain or have some level of physical discomfort.

You will know your Ringneck Parakeet better than anyone. If you think something is wrong with the bird, have him checked by a veterinarian. Most avian health problems can be diagnosed with blood and stool tests.

Common Health Issues in Ringneck Parakeets

The following health problems surface in companion birds of all species. It's imperative that you understand the warning signs of serious illness in your Ringneck Parakeet in order to get qualified veterinarian assistance for your pet.

Chlamydiosis

Chlamydiosis is also known as Psittacosis, this disease can be transferred from birds to humans. In the United States, there are about 100 to 200 cases reported annually in individuals who keep parrots, including parakeets and budgerigars.

The chlamydia psittaci bacteria is often transmitted by birds that are carriers, but have no overt signs of the illness. Transmission to humans occurs when the organism is inhaled from dried feces.

Symptoms in birds include a loss of appetite, weight loss, dehydration, fluffed out feathers, discharge from the nose and eyes, and green stools. The condition is often fatal.

Infected birds require treatment by a veterinarian. They will typically be given the antibiotic doxycycline by mouth, via injection, or dispensed in their food of water. The minimum treatment period is 45 days followed by re-testing 30 days later.

During the treatment period, extreme caution must be taken when cleaning the bird's cage, including wearing protective clothing.

The parakeet must be isolated from other birds during this time, and until the re-test shows it to be free of the disease.

In humans, the symptoms of Chlamydiosis contracted from pet birds present as flu like and are often referred to by the common name "Parrot Fever" which can be fatal.

If both you and your bird are sick, be sure to tell your doctor that you keep a parakeet. If you have not had the bird tested by a veterinarian, do so immediately.

Diarrhea

Diarrhea in pet birds can originate from a number of sources, but is most commonly the result of a change in diet, internal parasites and/or stress. Symptoms include loose stools and weight loss with ruffled feathers.

There are over-the-counter medications available (as an example Lambert Kay Pet Pectillin) to treat the problem at a cost of roughly $7 (£4.55).

If, however, there is no immediate improvement in the bird's condition, seek veterinary aid as dehydration can be fatal.

Feather Plucking

When a Ringneck Parakeet begins to pluck its own feathers, the bird is likely depressed or lonely.

Some degree of feather loss is a natural consequence of grooming, which leaves you to determine what is and is not excessive.

Bald patches are not normal, nor is bleeding, and both should be evaluated by an avian veterinarian.

Feather loss in some instances can signal more serious conditions like:

- feather cyst disease

- parasite activity

- allergies

- liver disease

- skin inflammation

- malnutrition

- skin dryness

- lack of sunlight and air

Try to evaluate the bird's overall condition in relation to the feather plucking, and give the animal more attention and more intellectual stimulation.

If, however, there is no improvement, or if the bird loses weight and/or stops eating, seek veterinary attention as the parakeet may be seriously ill.

Missing feathers can also be the result of aggression from a cage mate. If the affected bird has a cage companion, observe them closely to see if one is bullying the other.

Scaly Face and Leg Disease (Mites)

Mites present with white deposits on the bird's legs and feet, and around the beak and eyes is known as Scaly Face and Leg Disease. The condition is treated with oral or injected anti-parasitic medications.

It's important to medicate for mites immediately, as beak and leg deformities can result from long-term exposure to the parasites.

Aspergillosis

This is a respiratory illness caused by a fungal infection. It usually is only found in stressed birds that are kept in poor conditions.

Aspergillosis is extremely difficult to diagnosis, and even more difficult to treat because it is usually well advanced when discovered. Most diagnoses are speculative based on white cell counts derived from blood tests.

Treatments have to be tailored to the individual bird, so the aid of an avian veterinarian is crucial. The best defense against aspergillosis is keeping a clean, well-ventilated, well-lit environment for your parakeet.

Candidiasis

An overgrowth of yeast in the digestive tract causes an infection in the bird, commonly known as candidiasis. Symptoms include white lesions that appear around the mouth and throat.

The bird will show a loss of appetite and be subject to vomiting, and its crop will be slow to empty.

Yeast infections in parakeets can be treated successfully with anti-fungal medications from an avian veterinarian.

Pacheco's Disease

A group of herpes viruses cause this disease, which is almost always fatal and usually cannot be detected until it is too late to help the bird. The virus is spread by direct contact in feces, as an aerosol, or through food and water.

The disease damages the liver, spleen and kidneys. Symptoms include green feces, diarrhea, lack of appetite, listlessness, redness around the eyes, tremors and ruffled feathers.

Any parakeet that survives Pacheco's Disease will be infectious for life and cannot be kept in the same house with other birds.

In any bird that carries the virus, stress can cause an outbreak, even if the animal has been otherwise clinically "healthy."

There are actually more than 130 types of herpes viruses that can trigger illness in a wide variety of species, not just humans.

The herpes viruses that cause cold sores, genital herpes, chicken pox, shingles, Epstein-Barr, and mononucleosis are extremely widespread among humans and thus more commonly known.

While some herpes viruses are zoonotic, meaning they can pass between humans and animals, the viruses that cause Pacheco's Disease are not among them.

These viruses are naturally occurring among birds and are spread from a carrier bird to a new host. Some birds can carry one of the viruses throughout their lives and never become ill.

Proventricular Dilatation Disease (PDD)

Proventricular Dilatation Disease is a confounding medical disorder known popularly as "Parrot Wasting Syndrome."

It is characterized by vomiting, weight loss, a swollen crop and changes in the feces.

Although some birds are able to survive for months with veterinarian assistance, there is no treatment or cure, and PDD is ultimately fatal.

Parakeet Allergies in Humans

When parakeets flap their wings, preen, or defecate, debris or dander is spread in the air around them. Some of the dander is oily, and clings to surfaces while other types are dry and disperse widely.

Humans with an allergic sensitivity can easily come into contact with the dander, either when they touch an affected surface, or simply by breathing.

People with asthma are especially susceptible, but anyone sensitive to this irritant will experience a triggered immune response. The most typical symptoms are watery, itchy eyes, skin irritations and rashes and sometimes acute respiratory distress.

Much of the dander can be removed from the environment with daily cleaning of the bird's cage. However, even people with mild allergies may find this process too physically irritating to make keeping a pet bird in any way practical.

The source of the allergic reaction is the protein present in the bird's dander. All animals excrete different proteins, so a person who is allergic to a cat or a dog would not necessarily be allergic to a bird.

It's best to discuss the potential of adopting a bird with your doctor before getting a Ringneck Parakeet and undergoing allergy testing.

In order to help alleviate this problem, many bird owners successfully manage the presence of dander in their homes by using a vacuum cleaner equipped with a HEPA filter. Please do your research carefully if buying one as the efficiency varies considerably from brand to brand.

Parakeet Dander Pneumoconiosis

Some people suffer from extreme hypersensitivity to parakeet dander, which manifests as Parakeet Dander Pneumoconiosis or Allergic Alveolitis. With this condition the alveoli that line the human lungs are affected, reducing lung capacity.

Most people who are diagnosed with this condition have lived with birds for years and had an unusually high level of exposure to avian dander.

It may be 10 to 20 years before any clinical signs manifest, but once the disease is in motion, it can have an acute phase. This is characterized by chills, coughing, high fever and labored breathing.

In the sub-acute form, the sufferer must deal with a persistent dry cough and progressively diminished lung capacity.

If exposure continues, or no precautions are taken, more serious illnesses can result, like pulmonary fibrosis resulting in permanent lung damage.

Avian Influenza or Bird Flu

Since 2003, various species of birds in Asia, Europe and Africa have tested positive for the H5N1 Avian Influenza virus. This is a deadly zoonotic disease, which can be transferred to humans who come into contact with fecal matter produced by infected birds.

H5N1 is not a common threat in captive pet birds like Ringneck Parakeets. That being said, and in the interest of full disclosure, any bird can become infected with this virus, which is then easily passed to other birds and to people.

At this time, however, H5N1 in companion birds is not seen as a matter for serious concern. Instances of avian influenza have appeared most frequently in aquatic species, and in poultry kept in large, crowded, and often deplorable conditions.

As with any emerging pathogen, H5N1 is being closely monitored by health agencies around the world and cannot be completely dismissed in relation to any bird species. It would be advisable to check the up to date position before buying your companion bird.

Finding a Qualified Avian Veterinarian

Most small animal veterinarians are more accustomed to treating dogs and cats, and are drawn up short by the very different anatomy and health needs of a companion bird.

Locating a qualified avian veterinarian is extremely important for your bird's long-term health and well-being.

First, simply look in your local yellow pages or run an online search for avian veterinarians in your area.

You can also consult the home page of the Association of Avian Veterinarians (US) at www.aav.org or reach out to your state's Veterinary Medical Association.

In Europe the European Association of Avian Veterinarians at eaavonline.org is your most likely source for information.

When you have the name and contact information for a potential vet, schedule an office visit simply for interview purposes.

Make it clear that you are there to meet the vet and to discuss your bird and its care and that you are willing to pay for the visit.

Get answers to the following questions:

- How long have you been treating birds in your practice?

You want a professional who actually has a solid background in avian medicine, not just a vet who is willing to treat birds, but has little experience.

- Are you familiar with Ringneck Parakeets?

All species of birds have slightly different reactions to medicines and procedures. It is imperative that the vet you choose actually has experience with Ringneck Parakeets.

- To what veterinary associations do you belong?

In particular find out if the vet belongs to a group that specializes in the treatment of birds.

- Do you now or have you in the past had birds of your own?

While this is not an absolute requirement, it is helpful to work with a vet that has experience keeping companion birds. They are likely to be more tuned in to subtle signs of illness in your pet and be able to give practical advice.

- Does your practice make emergency care available after hours or do you recommend your clients to an emergency clinic with experience with birds?

Pets aren't any better at scheduling their mishaps and illnesses than humans. Make sure you have a resource to get medical attention for your bird at all hours of the day and night and on weekends and holidays.

- What are your fees?

Veterinarians are sensitive to the money that loving pet owners spend annually and all practices should happily provide a schedule of fees.

This allows you some opportunity to plan in advance for routine health care expenses for your bird, and can also lessen the "sticker shock" of any emergency care that might be needed.

- How often do you recommend checkups?

This will also give you a better idea of routine annual health care costs for your bird, and is a good baseline to judge how dedicated the vet in question will be to your pet's health. If you interview a vet who says, "Just come in when something is wrong," you need to keep looking!

- Do you make house calls?

Many avian veterinarians are agreeable to coming to your home for a higher fee because birds can get so stressed when traveling.

A bird that is already ill can be seriously harmed just by the anxiety of being taken out of its routine environment.

As already mentioned, before making the decision to bring a companion bird into your life, we strongly recommend that you take advice from your doctor and veterinarian so that you have a full understanding of any risks to your own health. We would also recommend ensuring that there are suitably qualified veterinarians in your area before buying your Ringneck Parakeet.

Let Your Bird Meet the Vet

If the initial interview goes well, schedule a second appointment so your bird can meet the vet. This will allow the vet to conduct a preliminary examination of the animal, but more importantly, it will allow you to watch how the vet relates to your pet and how your pet handles the situation.

How do the support staff in the clinic contribute to the visit and the exam? Is this an environment in which you will be comfortable, and into which you will willingly bring your bird? You need to have an easy, open, positive relationship with your veterinarian.

This is a person who could well be in a position of saving your parakeet's life someday. Everyone needs to get along and communicate well!

Don't Rule Out a Small Animal Vet

If you do not have access to an avian veterinarian, your bird still requires the services of a vet. You will have to go through the same interview process, and find a small animal vet who is not just open to treating your bird, but willing to learn more about the treatments the Ringneck Parakeet may require during its lifetime.

The best small animal vets to treat birds are those who have or who are willing to cultivate contact with avian veterinarians for long-distance consultations. These may be specialists teaching at a nearby college of veterinary medicine, or practicing vets in a larger town.

While it is more difficult to get care for your companion bird through a "regular" small animal vet, it is certainly not impossible.

Remember that these people became veterinarians because they love animals. When you find one who is willing to go the extra mile for your bird and expand their knowledge of avian medicine, you and your parakeet may have gained an invaluable ally.

Pet Insurance

Veterinary care, especially for birds, can become quite pricey. In addition to the fact that avian vets generally come with a higher price tag, you never know when an illness or injury will occur, resulting in expensive and unexpected costs.

With advances in veterinary care, today's pets can receive the same high quality care – such as chemotherapy for cancer and physical therapy for injuries – as their human counterparts. The cost of that care, however, can become quite hefty, making it essential for you to know how you plan to pay for veterinary care even before you bring your bird home.

Many pet owners have discovered that pet insurance helps defray the costs of veterinary expenses. Pet insurance is similar to health insurance in that you pay a monthly premium and a deductible and the pet insurance pays for whatever is covered in your plan, such as annual exams and blood work.

Shopping for pet insurance is similar to shopping for health insurance in the United States. As with health insurance, the age and the overall health of your Ringneck Parakeet will determine how much you will pay in premiums and deductibles. Ask plenty of questions to determine the best company and plan for your needs:

- Can you go to your regular vet, or do you have to go to a vet assigned by the pet insurance company?

- What does the insurance plan cover? Does it cover annual exams? Surgery? Emergency illness and injury?

- Does coverage begin immediately?

- Are pre-existing conditions covered? In addition, if your parakeet develops a health issue and you later have to renew the policy, is that condition covered when you renew your policy?

- Is medication covered?

- Do you have to have pre-authorization before your pet receives treatment? What happens if your bird has the treatment without pre-authorization?

- Does the insurance policy cover dental issues and chronic health problems, including any allergies?

- Is there a lifetime maximum benefit amount? If so, how much is that amount? A benefit plan with a lifetime maximum of only a few hundred dollars surely will not suffice for a parrot (or most pets, for that matter).

- Is there an excess limit i.e. an amount that you have to pay before the insurance pays out?

The above questions are not an exhaustive list but a good starting point. Take the time to research your pet insurance options and to consult a professional in this field. Compare the different plans available, what each covers, and the cost before making the decision on which is best for you and your pet.

Pet insurance may not be the answer for everyone. While pet insurance may not be a feasible option for you, consider having a backup plan, just in case your bird requires emergency care or you run into unexpected veterinarian costs.

A simple way to prepare for an emergency is to start a veterinary fund for your Ringneck Parakeet. Decide to put a certain amount of money aside each week, each month, or each paycheck to use in the case of an emergency. Think about the potential financial costs of veterinary care and plan for how you will pay for it now instead of waiting until something happens.

Chapter 5 - Care Sheet

Caution: Avoid the use of non-stick cookware and appliances in your home. The coating on these products can release fumes that are hazardous to your bird's health and potentially fatal.

Overview

Ringneck Parakeets are social birds with both emotional and physical needs. They have a lifespan of 20+ years and develop deep attachments to their humans.

As these birds can become very lonely, it is important to spend time with the bird, handling and playing with it daily.

Housing

A stainless steel or BPA-free plastic cage with horizontal bars spaced no more than 0.5 inches (1.3 centimeters). Minimum cage dimensions are 36 inches long x 24 inches deep x 48 inches high (91.4 centimeters x 61 centimeters x 122 centimeters)

The bottom of the cage should be lined with paper to facilitate daily cleaning but never with cat litter. Parakeets will eat the litter, which can be fatal.

Cage Placement

Choose an active part of the house that makes the bird feel like part of the family. Remember, you are your parakeet's "flock." Do not put the cage in direct sunlight, or subject the bird to a draft. Place the cage against a wall as high as your eye level.

Maintain a daytime temperature of between 60 F to 70 F / 15.6 C to 21.1 C and a night time temperature of no less than 40 F / 4.4 C. By covering the cage at night, it will help the parakeet to stay warmer.

Cage Cleaning

Change the bird's food and water daily and put down clean papers in the bottom of the cage. On a weekly basis, wash and disinfect the cage and all accessories with warm, soapy water. On a monthly basis, the cage should be dismantled and disinfected with vinegar and baking soda. Do not use cleaning chemicals and ensure any cleaning residue is thoroughly rinsed. Always allow all elements to dry thoroughly before putting the bird back inside its cage.

Transporting the Parakeet Outside the Home

Always use a secure travel crate and do not release the bird until you are inside a secondary enclosure like an aviary or a room with all the doors and windows closed. This includes taking the bird out of the cage at a veterinary clinic.

Cage Accessories

The parakeet's environment should include: ladders,

swings, perches, chewing and shredding toys, food and water dishes, bath, cuttlebone, mineral block and lava stone. The last three items are good chew toys that also keep the bird's beak worn down.

Do not buy perches covered in sandpaper. They irritate the bird's feet and increase the risk of infection.

Food

Parakeets do best on a diet of seed and nutritionally balanced pellet feeds. Give the bird fresh fruits and vegetables daily, removing uneaten bits within 2 hours.

Approximately 60% to 70% of the bird's diet should be bird pellets, with the remainder of the diet from fresh sources.

Choose dark, leafy vegetables, carrots, and broccoli. Beneficial fruits include kiwi, melon, apples, and pears.

Never give your parakeet apple seeds, rhubarb, cherry pits, or avocado. These items are toxic to parakeets. Again, check with your breeder or vet to see what may be particular to your area that should be avoided and for general advice on other foods that would be toxic to your bird.

Vitamins

Although Ringneck Parakeets should be able to get all they need nutritionally from a well-balanced diet, it's a good idea to provide them with a multivitamin in either pellet or liquid form.

Water

Both the bird's drinking and bath water should be de-chlorinated.

Socialization

Ringneck Parakeets are easy to tame, but they must be handled daily if they are to remain docile and friendly.

Signs of Ill Health

Don't mistake normal napping or sleeping time for sickness. Your bird will adapt to your waking and sleeping schedule (especially if you cover the cage at night), and will take short naps during the day.

Warning signs of potential illness include:

- swelling and / or discharge from the beak

- feathers that are fluffed out, missing or soiled

- sitting on the floor of the cage rather than perching

- coughing or wheezing

- stools that are discolored or runny

- favoring one foot

- discharge from the eyes or nostrils

- swelling of the eyes

- loss of appetite

Chapter 6 - Breeding

If you are interested in breeding Ringneck Parakeets, there's a bit more involved in the process than simply letting nature take its course. To state the obvious, parakeets aren't chickens.

The hens do follow their natural instinct to sit on a clutch of eggs and hatch them out, but from that point, things can go wrong. The breeder may have to step in and raise the chicks if the mother does not accept them.

Before you contemplate keeping a mated pair of Ringneck Parakeets, you should understand as much as possible about your role in their lives and that of their offspring.

The following is intended as a broad overview only. If you decide to move forward with the breeding of parakeet babies, you will need to conduct extensive research in the process and make sure that you have all the necessary supplies on hands. Little lives will be depending on you!

Methods for Breeding Ringneck Parakeets

Many Ringneck Parakeet enthusiasts become so interested in the birds that they want to breed them, especially in hopes of cultivating a new and beautiful color mutation.

There are two approaches to handling breeding pairs: housing the birds separately by gender and only bringing them together during mating season, or allowing two birds of opposite genders to occupy a cage for life.

Since parakeets are monogamous birds and bond deeply with their mates, it's important to make this decision first and stick with it. "Divorcing" a mated pair of Ringneck Parakeets is emotionally cruel to the birds.

Segregating Birds by Gender Before Mating Season

In a segregated situation, the breeder watches for the female to begin activity in the nesting box. At the first sign that she is interested, the male should be put near her enclosure, but not inside.

Females become aggressive during mating, and need a chance to get used to the male to minimize the chance of injuries occurring.

There are many varieties of nesting boxes for sale that provide a hen with the privacy she wants. Expect to pay $5 to $10 (£3.25 to £6.50) depending on the style you select.

Allow the male to remain outside the female's cage, but visible to her for about a week. A courtship ritual will occur through the bars of the two cages, with the male bowing to the female who will spend hours clinging to the cage near him.

When the male is introduced to her enclosure, the female will initiate the mating. The breeder should stay nearby to make sure the male isn't harmed. It is still possible that the pair will not bond, and that the male will have to be removed for his safety.

If, for any reason, the breeder wishes to keep the male and female paired even though there seems to be too much aggression for the male to be safe, both birds should be moved to a new cage in a different location.

This technique will force the two birds to develop a bond,

but it may also create the need to keep the two birds together permanently.

Creating Permanent Mated Pairs

Housing a mating pair for life is generally the preferred method of Ringneck Parakeet breeding because it cuts down on aggression.

Since these birds don't start to breed for the first time until they are 2 to 3 years of age, a pair housed together for at least a year will develop a strong bond.

This is good for the birds in many ways, since parakeets do have a tendency to get lonely. There will be obvious affection between the two birds, and in most cases you simply find the first egg in the nesting box.

Not only is permanent pairing better for the parakeets, but it allows the breeder to more accurately predict color mutations and to keep better records.

There are few worries about how the parents will care for the young, and in general, all parties concerned are just much happier.

Hatching Ringneck Parakeet Chicks

The egg of a Ringneck Parakeet is roughly the size of an American quarter (a ten pence coin in the UK), an approximate diameter of 2.4 centimeters or just under an inch.

Each egg will weigh about 0.32 ounces (9.1 grams). Of that weight, 7% is shell. These are very, very tiny babies!

The female will lay one white egg a day until the clutch is complete. Generally a Ringneck female lays 3 to 4 eggs, which will then require 22 to 24 days of incubation.

Some females will pluck a bald brood patch on their breast to make a warm spot for the eggs. This is a normal practice and nothing to be concerned about.

Most mating pairs will produce two clutches per year if the chicks are removed from their care at 10 to 15 days of age and raised by hand in a brooder. This allows the birds to be much more highly socialized.

Since the parents can no longer see the chicks once they are placed in the brooder, this is not a cruel practice, nor does it upset the adult birds.

If the parents raise the chick, expect a single clutch per year.

An incubating Ringneck Parakeet hen sits on the eggs with only brief pauses to move around and stretch or to eat. She will turn the eggs regularly, which allows for normal development of the embryo.

About two days before the chick is ready to hatch, it makes a small hole in the shell to gain more oxygen. The humidity in the cage should be increased slightly during this period, especially if you live in a dry climate. Simply misting the outside of the nesting box with a spray bottle should be sufficient.

When the chick is ready to emerge, it spends about 15 minutes creating a "hatch ring" round the egg. It then uses its legs to push apart the two sections of the shell. The hen will dispose of the shell, but if she does not, remove it so that it does not interfere with the next chick's hatching.

Note that the mother bird will be protective of her nest, and you may get pecked removing the shell, but not severely. Just move slowly, and do nothing to startle the bird or indicate a threat to her chick.

Caring for Ringneck Parakeet Chicks

If the hen does not care for the chick properly, you may have to hand feed the baby immediately. Newly hatched chicks must be fed every two hours around the clock.

If you find yourself in this situation and don't know what to do, get help from your vet or from a knowledgeable parakeet breeder in your area.

The first time you are responsible for a tiny, helpless chick completely on your own can be very stressful and frightening!

Experienced breeders generally have another female that will act as a foster parent, but if that is not an option, you will have to take over if the chick is to survive.

First, never handle the chick without disinfecting your hands first.

Be very, very, VERY gentle. Ringneck babies are incredibly delicate and fragile.

Chicks should be fed the first time six hours after hatching.

If the chick must be removed from the care of its parents, it should be housed in a brooder set at a temperature of 95 F / 35 C.

Any time a chick begins to pant, he is too warm and should be removed from the brooder to cool down. Decrease the temperature 1 degree at a time until the chick appears comfortable.

If the chicks huddle together under the center of the lamp, they are too cold. Follow the same procedure of increasing the temperature one degree at a time.

To hand feed a Ringneck Parakeet chick, you will need a plastic pipette, a syringe, or an eye dropper. Each of these items will cost roughly $1 (£0.65).

Always have the supplies on hand to hand feed chicks before the eggs start to hatch. Better to be safe than to be left without the things you need in the middle of the night or on a weekend.

What is a Brooder?

A brooder is a contained area where baby chicks can be raised apart from their parents. It does not have to be purchased and can even be made from a sturdy cardboard box.

The important thing is that the babies not be subjected to drafts. Maintaining constant temperature in the box is critical.

Always have a digital thermometer on hand in case you have to quickly construct a brooding box at the last minute. Thermometers cost roughly $7 to $10 (£4.55 to £6.50). The normal type of heat source used is an electric heating element or heat lamp suspended over the area. The best devices are those with thermostats that can be regulated.

If you are using a heat lamp, make sure you have a back-up bulb in case one burns out. Both infrared and clear lights work equally well.

Heat lamps with thermostats are available in a price range of $35 to $50 (£22.75 to £32.50) with replacement bulbs averaging

$10 to $15 (£6.50 to £9.75). Please invest in a specialist heat lamp to reduce the risk of fires and always use the equipment as per the manufacturers instructions.

Hand Feeding Day Old Chicks

Never force a chick to eat if it refuses to do so and never overfill the crop. You have to be able to identify this bit of avian anatomy to successful hand feed a chick.

The crop is a chamber between the bird's esophagus and stomach where food is held and partially digested before it passes farther down the digestive tract. It is clearly visible in young chicks because they have no feathers.

The first time a chick is fed, use an electrolyte solution like Pedialyte (or a similar infant formula) or an Oral Rehydration Solution (ORS) in the UK. This will ensure that the baby's digestive system is working properly.

After the first feeding, you should switch to a commercial hand feeding formula prepared at a temperature of 105 F to108 F / 40.6 C to 42.2 C.

During the first few feedings, only a couple of drops will be necessary.

Feed every two hours after that, observing the chick's crop.

It should be almost empty at the end of every two-hour period.

When feeding, gently place a single drop of solution on the LEFT side of the chick's mouth. If the chick refuses food, place it back in the brooder and wait 15 minutes before you try again.

Hand Feeding Formula

Kaytee Exact is a widely used hand feeding formula for baby birds. It was the first "instant" formula to appear on the market and is extremely well respected.

Prepare the mixture EXACTLY according to the instructions on the box.

18 oz. / 0.51 kg. sells for about $10 (£6.50). Again, it is best to have this product on hand just in case.

Kaytee is not the only infant formula available for baby birds. You may also want to research comparable products made by ZuPreem, LeFeber and inTune.

Please note that the Kaytee site includes a very good tutorial page on hand feeding baby birds with included videos. The site also maintains an "Ask the Experts" section. This is a good resource to understand more about hand feeding, which can be an intimidating prospect for those new to aviculture.

You can visit:

www.kaytee.com/pet-birds/general-care/hand-feeding.htm

As Your Ringneck Chick Grows

As the Ringneck chicks grow and develop, watch their crops to determine how often they should be fed.

When the birds are down to two hand feedings a day, they will begin to refuse their formula, generally by slinging it around. This is the time to begin to wean the chicks.

Even though they have been refusing their formula, the fledglings may lose a little weight in the transition to regular food. This can go on for two weeks and will worry the life out of you. Be prepared!

This point cannot be stressed strongly enough. DO NOT force feed a baby bird.

The fledgling will accept solid foods in time. If it continues to beg for hand feeding, one feeding a day will be sufficient to meet its nutritional needs.

You are grappling with a psychological dependency in the bird, not a physical need.

Give the chick lots of attention but continue to offer solid foods by hand. They will get the idea, but you may be shocked at just how stubborn these birds can be! If you are struggling, seek advice from your veterinarian or breeder.

The Practice of Leg Banding

People who breed Ringneck Parakeets for sale customarily put a closed leg band on the hatchlings that is engraved with the breeder's initials, the place where the bird was bred, the year of hatching, and a unique identifying number.

Some owners have the band removed if it is irritating the bird's leg or getting caught on parts of the cage. Never try to remove a band on your own in this event. A special tool is required to do the job properly. Go to an avian veterinarian a bird shop, or seek the aid of another breeder who has the correct equipment.

A Final Word on Breeding and Raising Chicks

At best, this is a broad overview of the process of breeding Ringneck Parakeets and raising parakeet chicks.

Before you attempt this complicated and labor-intensive process, learn everything you can and talk to other parakeet breeders, either in person or online.

There is no such thing as being over-prepared to raise a clutch of parakeet chicks for the first time!

Make sure that you completely understand everything that is involved and have all the necessary supplies on hand.

Parakeet chicks are tiny, fragile creatures that will depend entirely on you for everything they need.

Even the most experienced breeders admit to harrowing moments caring for these little darlings.

Make no mistake, raising baby Ringnecks is a wonderfully rewarding experience, but it is hard work and can be emotionally draining, especially if you're doing it for the first time.

Do not go into the process on a whim, and make sure you have a good source of advice and counsel from either a qualified avian vet or a breeder or community of breeders you can turn to for advice.

Please also bear in mind the enormous amount of time and commitment required to safely undertake breeding of the wonderful creatures. It is not for the faint hearted!

Chapter 7 - Life After You

Sometimes life takes unexpected turns. If you have ever volunteered at or have been to an animal shelter, you have likely heard the heartbreaking stories of some of the homeless dogs, cats, birds, rabbits and other animals. Their beloved human has passed away and they are now at the shelter, confused and depressed. Countless pets languish in animal shelters and rescues after their owner dies because the person failed to make plans for their pet's future without them.

Most people expect to outlive their pets by many years. But, that does not always happen. What will happen to your parrot once you are gone? Parakeets have a much longer lifespan than most pets, so that is a question you really want to think about and answer now. If something happens to you, you want to know that your bird will be properly cared for and loved.

Some cell phones allow you to input an ICE (In Case of Emergency) number with notes. If your cell phone has such an option, I recommend that you use it. Alternatively, you might find it easier to write the following information on a piece of a paper and put it in your wallet with your driver's license. You can also give a copy of this information to your neighbors along with friends and family. The list should include:

- The names of each of your pets, including your Ringneck Parakeet

- The names and phone numbers of family members or friends who have agreed to temporarily care for your pets in an emergency.

- The name and phone number of your veterinarian.

Be sure to also talk with your neighbors, letting them know how many pets you have and the type of pets. That way, if something happens to you, they can alert the authorities, ensuring your pets do not linger for days before they are found.

If you fail to do that and something happens to you, someone will find your pet and will have questions: What is his name? What does he eat? How old is he? To make sure your bird is not forgotten in the case of an emergency, ask several friends or family members to be responsible for taking care of him temporarily should something happen to you.

Even before something happens, prepare instructions for the intended temporary guardians, providing amended instructions as necessary. Also, if you are happy to do so, provide each individual with a key to your home. Remember to let your home insurer know you have done so and ask them to confirm that does not affect your coverage. Instructions should include:

- The name and phone numbers of each individual who agreed to temporarily take care of your parrot and other pets.

- Your Ringneck Parakeet's diet and feeding schedule, so he can maintain his normal schedule.

- The name and phone number of your avian veterinarian.

- Any health problems and medications your bird may take on a daily basis, including dosage instructions, instructions on how to give the medicine, and where the medicine is kept.

- Information on the care of your parrot, such as when he typically sleeps, how much time he generally gets out of the cage, and so on.

Put as much information as necessary to ensure the temporary guardians can provide the same level of care to which your Ringneck Parakeet is accustomed.

Finding a Permanent Home

Ensure your bird's future by finding a permanent home for him in case of your unexpected incapacity or death. Here are some things to keep in mind when considering a new home for your beloved friend in the event of your death:

- Consider family members and friends who love animals and have successfully cared for pets themselves. You may have a particular family member, for example, who is fond of your Ringneck Parakeet and vice-versa.

- How many pets do you have? If you have a pair of Ringneck Parakeets, do not split them up if at all possible. Breaking up a pair could result in great distress, including self-mutilation, feather plucking and screaming.

- Is the person you are considering willing to care for a parrot, regardless of how long he lives? He may even outlive his new guardian.

- Find an alternate new guardian in case something happens and the first one is unable to care for your pet as intended.

Always remain in contact with the potential new guardian to ensure he or she is still able or willing to care for your bird (and other pets) in case of an emergency. If one person backs out, you can then take the time necessary to find another potential permanent guardian.

Making it Legal

Once you have found the best caregiver, consult with a lawyer or a solicitor. The lawyer/solicitor can create a legal agreement, whether a will or a trust, that is based on what you want for your pet in the case of your unexpected death.

A will can dictate who your bird is to live with upon your death while you can place funds – to help pay for the ongoing care of your Ringneck Parakeet – in a trust that the guardian can use to help care for him.

Another alternative is to take out a suitable life insurance policy which can be written under trust for your pet's guardian. This is a complex area and I recommend you take specialist advice.

While it is not the most pleasant topic to talk or to think about it, it is extremely important to your pet's continued well-being that you address what is to happen to him and who will take care of him before that time comes.

You may also want to consider what you would do in the event that you had an accident or became ill. Are friends and relatives able to step in at a moment's notice to look after your beloved companion?

Chapter 8 – Closing Thoughts

P arakeets and budgies are the most popular of all companion bird species, in part due to their manageable size, but also because they are intelligent and affectionate creatures.

Ringneck Parakeets have lived in companionship with humans for centuries, frequenting the palaces of the Romans and the salons of aristocrats and intelligentsia across Europe.

The birds are so adaptable they have become naturalized in the United Kingdom, thriving in a climate well north of their lands of origin in Asia China and Africa.

When kept as a pet, a parakeet may be a presence in the life of its owner for 20 years or more, amassing a working vocabulary of words, recognizing members of the family, and even grieving if someone in its human "flock" dies.

Rescue groups routinely place birds who have survived their elderly caretakers, a problem even more serious in larger parrots like macaws that can live to almost 100 years of age in captivity.

The perception that a pet bird simply sits in a cage is both naive and cruel. Parakeets need companionship as well as intellectual and physical stimulation. They must be allowed to be what they are — birds — which means free time outside their cages.

You will never "house train" a parakeet. They do what they need to do when and where they need to do it. You will be cleaning the bird's cage daily, and there will be accidents when it is out and free flying in a "bird safe" room (one where there is no means of escape and hazards are minimized).

Keeping a pet bird is labor intensive, and it's not a proposition to be taken up lightly. Some people, though they might enjoy interacting with birds, simply are not up to the task of keeping one in their homes. This is a decision you must make before you even consider buying a parakeet and bringing it home. Keeping a parakeet should NEVER be an impulse decision.

Use all available resources to find out what it's really like to live with a pet parakeet before you take the plunge. The Internet has made this a fairly simple task, not only with a wealth of resource information, but also with discussion forums dedicated to all kinds of bird husbandry.

This book has attempted to provide a comprehensive overview of life with a Ringneck Parakeet. You should now have a working understanding of what these lovely little creatures need, and be in possession of enough of the "lingo" to ask the right questions as you move forward or back away as the case may be.

Living with a pet of any kind isn't just a matter of personal pleasure, but also a tremendous responsibility. The animals we bring into our lives and hearts depend on us entirely to do for them what they cannot do for themselves.

Our reward is not only their unconditional love and loyalty, but also the opportunity to gain daily insight into how another living creature perceives and interacts with the world.

If you have never had a companion bird, and you believe you can be what a Ringneck Parakeet needs of its human, you won't regret your decision. There's a reason why these birds are the most popular of all the avian companion species — they're simply amazing and endlessly fun.

Chapter 9 - Frequently Asked Questions

Are parakeets and budgies the same bird?

The term "parakeet" is applied to slender-bodied parrots with long tails. The word is not used precisely, and it can get even more confusing when applied to budgies, which are indeed parakeets . . . but not all parakeets are budgies!

In pet stores, the birds that are often labeled "parakeets" are actually budgerigars. A good way to immediately tell the difference is that budgies have stripes on their heads and Ringneck Parakeets don't.

Shouldn't I really have two birds? Won't one be lonely?

The decision to have one or two birds has to depend on your ability to care for them. It is true that parakeets are not solitary creatures. They are flock animals, and, in the absence of another bird to keep him company, you will be your pet's "flock."

If you can't spend a lot of time interacting with your parakeet, playing with your pet, and showing him the attention and affection he needs, you may need to reconsider keeping a bird at all.

Getting a second parakeet should never be a substitute for developing a relationship with the first bird.

If you do get a second bird, keep it in a separate cage in another part of the house for at least two weeks to ensure it is completely healthy before allowing the two parakeets to meet.

During that time, work on bonding with the second bird. With two parakeets, you're really something of a flock "manager." You want to have a loving relationship with both of your pets, and you want them to bond.

Really think about what you're doing getting a second bird. What is your motivation? Don't forget to factor in the double maintenance time and double the responsibility.

Where should I put my bird's cage and how should I set it up?

Ringneck Parakeets like activity. You don't want to put the cage in the middle of the room, which will just make the bird feel anxious, but one wall of the living room is an ideal choice.

Avoid direct sunlight and all drafts. Parakeets don't tolerate rapid changes in temperature.

Also, make sure the cage is reasonably high off the ground. After all, birds live in trees and they don't feel secure at low levels where they would naturally be vulnerable to predators. Putting the cage at roughly your eye level works well because not only will it make the bird feel safe, it will facilitate your interaction with your new pet.

Should parakeets have time out of the cage?

Absolutely! Parakeets love to fly. Stretching their wings is good for them, physically and emotionally. Your bird needs exercise and intellectual stimulation to be happy.

Create a bird safe room with play areas to which the bird will naturally gravitate. This will help to control the amount of droppings you have to clean up.

Always make sure the parakeet has access to clean food and water inside and outside of its cage. Use only dechlorinated water with your pet.

I'd like to get my parakeet some toys. What should I buy?

Providing your parakeet with toys will not only keep the bird happy and entertained, it will help him keep his beak and claws worn down naturally.

Birds like things with shiny surfaces, and are fond of toys they can manipulate with their beaks and claws.

Ringneck Parakeets are problem solvers by nature and are happiest when they're "working" at something.

Are there toys that I shouldn't buy because they're dangerous?

As with most pets, anything with small parts that could be swallowed is a choking hazard and should be avoided.

Also beware of toys that contain plastics. Make sure they say "BPA free" and are non-toxic to ensure your bird isn't being exposed to poisonous chemicals.

Should my parakeet drink tap water?

Parakeets are much more vulnerable to impurities and chemicals in water than humans. Give your bird only dechlorinated water. Your best option is pure spring water.

Clean your pet's dish and bath daily, so harmful bacteria does not begin to grow in either receptacle.

How frequently do parakeets defecate?

On average, a parakeet will produce waste materials every 12 - 15 minutes. Young birds defecate more frequently. This is, without question, the most challenging aspect of parakeet maintenance for you, especially when the birds are out of the cage for free flight time.

The liner of your bird's cage will need to be cleaned daily, with more thorough washing and disinfecting weekly and monthly.

For time out of the cage, create a bird safe room that is not only secured against possible escape, but that can be easily cleaned. Hardwood, tiled or linoleum floors are much better than carpet or rugs!

How warm should I keep my house so my parakeet won't get cold?

During the day, don't let your home get cooler than 60 F to 70 F / 15.6 C to 21.1 C. The minimum at night is no cooler than 40 F / 4.4 C. You can also cover the cage at night to help your bird stay warmer.

Don't subject your parakeet to rapid changes in temperature, and avoid placing his cage in a drafty spot or in direct sunlight.

Do parakeets need a lot of sleep?

Your Ringneck Parakeet will quickly adapt to your own rhythm of sleep. Dim the lights a few minutes before you're ready to turn in, and the bird will begin to settle down.

For young birds, leave a night light on in the room since they tend to panic in total darkness.

Since parakeets do wake with the first light of morning, you will want to cover their cage at night to cut down on their tendency to be your very own feathered alarm clock.

During the day, your Ringneck will take several little naps, dozing on his perch. If all the time were to be added up, he probably gets about 10 to 12 hours of sleep in every 24 hour cycle.

How can I recognize signs of sickness in my Ringneck Parakeet, and what should I do about it?

If your parakeet sleeps for hours in a single day, and if its feathers are puffed out, you have reason to be concerned. Birds try to hide signs of illness as a survival mechanism. If they look sick, they also look vulnerable and weak to larger, predatory animals.

If your Ringneck is not vigilant, alert, and interested in

what's going on around him, he may not be feeling well. Put a specialist heating lamp near the cage to provide a little extra warmth, but don't let the situation go on for more than a day without seeking the help of a veterinarian.

Why should I buy my Macaw from a reputable breeder?

In 1973 the Convention on International Trade in Endangered Species of Wild Fauna and Flora (CITES) was established to combat over–exploitation. You can get more information at this website www.cites.org. Sadly, many baby parrots are stolen from their nests, sold and smuggled into the Unites States and other countries where they can command higher prices.

When you begin to look for your own bird, it's important to work with reputable breeders who maintain active aviaries. Be cautious of anyone who has a single bird for sale. Try to find out the parrot's origin before making a purchase. Your desire is to support the species, not the illegal trade in exotic animals. Please exercise extreme caution when buying your companion bird online. This can expose them to dangerous conditions when being shipped and you must ensure that this has been addressed by the breeder and carrier.

If you are interested in actively supporting the conservation of parrot species in the wild, see the World Parrot Trust's website at www.parrots.org.

Chapter 10 - Relevant Websites

When you start looking around the internet it can take some time to track down exactly what you are looking for.

A one-stop shop for all your parrot needs is what is required and the sites below offer you the convenience of pulling together many of the best products from around the web.

Enjoy Shopping!

Shopping

United States of America Website

www.tropicalbirdshop.com

United Kingdom Website

www.tropicalbirdshop.co.uk

Associations

British Trust for Ornithology: Ring-necked Parakeet

http://blx1.bto.org/birdfacts/results/bob7120.htm

The Aviculture Society (UK)

www.avisoc.co.uk

World Parrot Trust: Ringneck Parakeet

www.parrots.org/index.php/encyclopedia/profile/ringneck
_parakeet/

World Parrot Trust: Gallery of Photos

www.parrots.org/index.php/parrotgallery/category/C132/

Indian Ringneck - Learn About Your Feathered Family
Member!

www.IndianRingneck.com

PETCO Ringneck Parakeet Care Sheet

www.petco.com/caresheets/bird/Parakeet_Ringneck.pdf

Bird Breeders Discussion Forum (US)

http://birdbreeders.com

Bird Trader (UK)

www.birdtrader.co.uk

National Cage Bird Show (US)

www.ncbs.org

North American Parrot Society (US)

www.northamericanparrotsociety.com

The Society of Parrot Breeders and Exhibitors (US)

www.spbe.org

Association of Avian Veterinarians (US)

www.aav.org

Aviculture Society of Australia

www.birds.org.au

Parrot Society of New Zealand

www.parrot.co.nz

World Parrot Trust

www.parrots.org

Avian Web

www.avianweb.com

Video and Audio

The Internet Bird Collection

- Male feeding a Senegal parrot (video).

http://ibc.lynxeds.com/video/rose-ringed-parakeet-psittacula-krameri/male-feeding-senegal-parrot-tree

- Male perched on a branch feeding (video).

http://ibc.lynxeds.com/video/rose-ringed-parakeet-psittacula-krameri/bird-perched-branch-feeding

- Female parakeet bathing on the ground next to a sprinkler (video).

http://ibc.lynxeds.com/video/rose-ringed-parakeet-psittacula-krameri/female-taking-bath-ground-next-sprinkler

- Two Ringneck Parakeets calling (audio).

http://ibc.lynxeds.com/sound/rose-ringed-parakeet-psittacula-krameri/two-birds-calling

Kingtutone Channel on YouTube

An Indian Ringneck Parrot Hatching

http://youtu.be/LurTNqa0Bgk

"How to teach a bird to talk, a step by step tutorial"
www.youtube.com/watch?v=o3oE_8EJa-E

Glossary

Allergy – A sensitivity in some individuals to foreign substances like bird dander that elicit negative immune responses such as itching, watering eyes, sneezing and respiratory distress. All allergies vary in magnitude. Pet allergies are specific to the proteins present in the dander of the given species and are not necessarily universal.

Avian specialist – A professional who specializes in the care of birds and is generally a veterinarian.

Aviary bird – Any bird held in captivity in a large outside enclosure. Birds that live in these circumstances may or may not be routinely handled by humans.

Beak - On birds, the upper and lower mandibles or jaws form the "beak," which, in Ringneck Parakeet, has a hook shape.

Beaking – A behavior typical in parrots and other birds in which the bird uses its bill to explore something that has attracted its interest. People who are not familiar with birds often mistake beaking as an attempt to bite. The behavior is, however, an expression of curiosity, not aggression.

Bird fancier's lung – This is an alternate name for hypersensitivity pneumonitis, an allergic disease that develops in bird owners after years of exposure to bird dander. There may be few symptoms beyond a dry cough in the early stages of the conditions, but if chronic, it can present with a fever, chills, and seriously diminished respiratory capacity. If left untreated, it can result in permanent lung damage.

Bluffing — In adolescent Ringneck Parakeets, this is anti-social and aggressive behavior due to hormone imbalances normally present in the maturation process. Typically the behavior resolves in four months to a year.

Breast - The area of a bird's body located just below the throat.

Cere - This is the area of flesh located above a bird's beak where the openings for the nostrils are located.

Crop - A sac-like organ located between the parakeet's esophagus and stomach. It serves as a kind of "first stomach" to perform preliminary digestion.

Crown - The term to describe the top portion of a bird's head.

Ear - A bird's ears should be invisible most of the time, hidden under a thin layer of feathers. The two small ear openings are located on either side of the animal's head, just behind the eyes.

Eyes - In order to provide a maximum field of vision, a bird's eyes are located on either side of its head.

Fear aggression — Biting and other aggressive behaviors exhibited by animals, including birds, in response to any event that has frightened the creature.

HEPA filter - HEPA is the acronym for "High Efficiency Particulate Air" filter. When used with a vacuum cleaner, a HEPA filter can remove 99.97% of all particles in the air as small as just tens of a micrometer. HEPA filters are extremely useful in controlling levels of pet dander present in a household.

Imitative speech – It is largely thought that the kind of speech in which parrots engage is imitative, simply reflecting their ability to repeat what they have heard.

Many parrot owners, however, insist that their birds understand and respond appropriately with their acquired vocabularies.

Learned aggression – Behaviors that are aggressive in nature, including biting. Learned and used by an animal to illicit predictable and desired responses.

Mantle - The descriptive term for a bird's back.

Nape - The descriptive term for the back of a bird's neck.

Nictating membrane - A thin, semi-transparent "third" eyelid that passes over the surface of a bird's eye like a squeegee to protect and clean the surface of the eye.

Parrot – All birds belonging to the family Psittacidae. Generally these birds are tropical in origin, brightly colored, and have short, hooked beaks. All parrots, including parakeets, are known for their ability to mimic sounds including human speech.

Parrot fever – A disease in humans caused by the bacterium Chlamydia psittaci which can be fatal.

Pet bird – Also referred to as "companion birds." Any bird that lives with and interacts with humans on a daily basis.

Primary feathers - The ten long wing feathers that allow a Ringneck Parakeet to fly.

Responsive speech – A description for parrot speech that appears to be responsive in that the bird gives the "correct" answer to a question, however, the response itself has been learned and is therefore "canned."

Rump - The area beneath the bird's primary flight feathers located on the parakeet's lower back.

Secondary feathers - The feathers of the wing under the primary feathers that are placed closer to the body.

Speech training – Any training that is designed to teach a parrot to "talk" so that the bird will be able to utter given words and phrases.

Syrinx - The rough equivalent of vocal chords in humans. A flexible structure in the throat of a Parakeet that allows the bird to talk and vocalize.

Territorial aggression – Any aggressive behavior exhibited by animals, including birds, triggered by someone or something invading or coming too close to what the creature perceives to be its territory.

Training aids – Any device used to help a human teach or train an animal, including a bird, to exhibit a desired behavior or to give a desired response, such as speech in parrots and parakeets.

Trick training – Any means of training that is designed to teach an animal, including a bird, some desired behavior that is executed according to a learned cue.

Vent - The area under a bird's tail feathers for elimination. Birds defecate, but they do not urinate.

Zoonotic – A disease that can be transmitted from an animal to a human being.

Index

D

E

F

G

H

I

L

Photo Credits

Cover Design:- Liliana Gonzalez Garcia, www.ipublicidades.com (info@ipublicidades.com)

Inside Cover Page By Richard Taylor
(originally posted to Flickr as IMG_6777) [CC-BY-2.0 http://commons.wikimedia.org/wiki/File%3APsittacula_kra meri_-
Canberra_Walk_In_Aviary%2C_Canberra%2C_Australia-8a.jpg

Page 4 By Christine Matthews
Ring Necked Parakeet (Psittacula krameri), Kew Gardens for TQ1876. This work is licensed under the Creative Commons Attribution-Share Alike 2.0 Generic Licence. www.geograph.org.uk/photo/3202897

Page 9 By Deedles47 (Own work) [CC-BY-SA-3.0 http://commons.wikimedia.org/wiki/File%3AIndian_Ringn eck_Parakeets_in_Bakersfield%2C_California.JPG

Page 27 By Eric C Bryan
www.flickr.com/photos/flowers-of-the-sea/5196549370/sizes/n/

Page 45 By Jim Linwood
www.flickr.com/photos/brighton/4271744512/sizes/n/

Page 57 By Richard Taylor
(originally posted to Flickr as IMG_6777)
http://commons.wikimedia.org/wiki/File%3APsittacula_kra
meri_-
Canberra_Walk_In_Aviary%2C_Canberra%2C_Australia-
8a.jpg

Page 59 By Vase Petrovski from Skopje, Macedonia
(Indi in motion Uploaded by snowmanradio) [CC-BY-2.0
http://commons.wikimedia.org/wiki/File%3APsittacula_kra
meri_-yellow_mutation_-flying-9.jpg

Page 86 By P G Palmer (AU)
www.flickr.com/photos/pgpalmer_au/6867782101/sizes/n/

Page 92 By Ajith Chatie
www.flickr.com/photos/36008503@N03/3801281948/sizes/m

Page 105 By Eric C Bryan
www.flickr.com/photos/flowers-of-the-
sea/6350899587/sizes/n/

Page 111 By Doegox
www.flickr.com/photos/doegox/480079995/sizes/n/

Page 114 By Loren Sztajer
www.flickr.com/photos/lorensztajer/5394011631/sizes/n/

Page 116 By Eajslater (Own work)
http://commons.wikimedia.org/wiki/File%3AFeral_Ring-necked_Parakeet.jpg

Page 115 Photo courtesy www.tropicalbirdshop.com

All Creative Commons work

These works are licensed under the Creative Commons Attribution 3.0 Unported License. To view a copy of this license, visit http://creativecommons.org/licenses/by/3.0/ or send a letter to Creative Commons, 444 Castro Street, Suite 900, Mountain View, California, 94041, USA.

All other photos – www.bigstockphotos.com

References

Petco: Ringneck Parakeet Care Sheet

http://www.petco.com/caresheets/bird/Parakeet_Ringneck.pdf

Indian Ring-Necked Parakeet

http://www.drsfostersmith.com/pic/article.cfm?aid=1549

Animal Pest Alert: Indian Ringneck Parakeet

http://www.agric.wa.gov.au/objtwr/imported_assets/content/pw/vp/bird/pestnoteindianringneckfinaltext_200607.pdf

Jordan, Theresa. "Introduction to Ringneck Parakeets."

http://www.birdsnways.com/wisdom/ww13eiv.htm

Indian Ringneck Parrot

http://www.avianweb.com/indianringneck.html

World Parrot Trust: Ringneck Parakeet

http://www.parrots.org/index.php/encyclopedia/profile/ringneck_parakeet/

BBC News. "How Do Parakeets Survive in the UK?"

http://news.bbc.co.uk/1/hi/magazine/6478911.stm

Hayward, Jim. "Ringneck Parakeet, Indian (Psittacula krameri manillensis)"

http://www.parrotmag.com/breeding/56-ringneck-parakeet-indian-psittacula-krameri-manillensis

British Garden Birds: Ring-necked Parakeet

http://www.garden-birds.co.uk/birds/ring-necked_parakeet.htm

Moustakki, Nikki. Parakeets for Dummies. April 23, 2007. Kindle Edition.

O'Connor, Rebecca K. "10 Facts About Living with Parrots."

http://www.birdchannel.com/bird-species/find-the-right-bird/facts-about-parrots.aspx

The Basics of Living with a Parrot

http://jamiesparrothelp.wordpress.com/2011/12/16/the-basics-of-living-with-a-parrot/

Indian Ringnecks as Pets

http://www.indianringneck.com/pet/

Baum, Joyce. "Breeding Indian Ringnecks."

http://www.birdsnways.com/wisdom/ww57e.htm

Notes:

Lightning Source UK Ltd.
Milton Keynes UK
UKOW06f1420210917

309618UK00009B/46/P